LEWISTON CITY LIBRARY
428 Thain
Lewiston, Idaho 83501
(208) 743-6519

DATE DUE

JAN 0 2 1998	
JAN 2 6 1998	
FEB 1 3 1998	
MAR 0 4 1998	
APR 0 1 1998	
SEP 1 2 1998	
JAN 2 9 2000	

WITHDRAWN FROM
LEWISTON CITY LIBRARY

PRINTCRAFT

Stetson Hats
and the John B. Stetson Hat Company
1865-1970

Jeffrey B. Snyder

4880 Lower Valley Road, Atglen, PA 19310

Dedicated to the memory of Chaucer Hall

Snyder, Jeffrey B.
    Stetson hats and the John B. Stetson Hat Company, 1865-1970 / Jeffrey B. Snyder.
       p.   cm.
    Includes bibliographical references and index.
    ISBN 0-7643-0211-6 (hardcover)
    1. John B. Stetson Hat Company--History. 2. Hat Trade--United States--History.
  3. Hats--Collectors and collecting--United States.
  I. Title.
HD9948.U64J647   1997
338.7'6874'0973--dc21   97-5257
                                                                          CIP

Copyright © 1997 by Schiffer Publishing, Ltd.

All rights reserved. No part of this work may be reproduced or used in any form or by any means—graphic, electronic, or mechanical, including photocopying or information storage and retrieval systems—without written permission from the copyright holder.

ISBN: 0-7643-0211-6

Book Design by Joy Shih & Blair Loughrey

Printed in Hong Kong

About the Values in This Book

Please note: The value ranges that appear here in the captions for Stetson hats are derived from compiled sources and were not supplied by the people acknowledged in the credit lines. The ranges were conscientiously determined to reflect the market at the time this work was compiled. No responsibility for their future accuracy is accepted by the author, the publisher, or the people credited with the photographs.

Stetson is a registered trademark of the John B. Stetson Company. The John B. Stetson Company did not authorize this book nor furnish or approve any of the information contained therein. This book is derived from the author's independent research.

The black and white cover photograph depicts men working in the Stetson factory sizing department in the 1920s. This photograph was provided courtesy of the Pennsylvania State Archives.

> Published by Schiffer Publishing Ltd.
> 4880 Lower Valley Road
> Atglen, PA 19310
> Phone: (610) 593-1777; Fax: (610) 593-2002
> Please write for a free catalog.
> This book may be purchased from the publisher.
> Please include $2.95 for shipping.
> Try your bookstore first.

We are interested in hearing from authors with book ideas on related subjects.

Looking for Stetson Material

The author continues to look for catalogs, advertisements, tales of former employees or salesmen, and of course vintage Stetson hats to include in upcoming revisions to this text. Jeffrey B. Snyder may be contacted through Schiffer Publishing, Ltd. I thank you in advance for your interest and cooperation.

Contents

Acknowledgments 4
Introduction 5
    Basic Definitions
    Who Wore Stetson Hats?
    The World's Most Expensive Hat
    Amazing Claims of Strength
    "Hats Not All Folks!"

Chapter I. Stetson Hats and Hat Manufacturing 26
    Stetson Hat Identification
    Manufacturing Felt Hats

Chapter II. The History of John B. Stetson and His Company 48
    The Early Years — 1830-1870
    Stetson Company Boom Years — 1870-1920
    The Middle Years — 1920-1947
    The Long Slide to Licensing — 1948-1971
    Stetson Lives On

Chapter III. Men's Hats 72
    Hats of East and West — 1870-1920
    Hats From 1920 Onward
    Hat Etiquette For Men

Chapter IV. Women's Hats 132
    Women's Hats From 1870-1920
    Women's Hats From 1920 Onward

Chapter V. Care of Hats 174
    Searching for and Evaluating Hats
    Caring for Hats
    Handling Hats

Conclusion 177
Endnotes 178
Bibliography 183
Appendix 185
Index 186

Acknowledgments

Courtesy of Lynn Trusdell.

A book project such as this is never a solo effort. Many people provided invaluable information and ready access to their personal collections or shop stock. I wish to thank them all. Without their help, this text would never have been possible. My heartfelt thanks is extended to Mark Arrowsmith of Arrowsmith's Relics of the Old West ..., Irene Centofanti, W.D. Clarke, Cowboy Trader Gallery, Peggy A. DeAngelo, Elmer and Jan Diederich, Paul Dormont, Dick Engel, Rick Ewig—Assistant Director of the Reference Department of the American Heritage Center of the University of Wyoming, Ray Huffman, Jack Laura, Bruce Mackinnon, William R. Morris, Gregory S. Ng, Joy Shih Ng, Joan Palicia, Larry and Marylin Robinson, Peter Schubert, Charlie and Karla Smith, Desire Smith, James J. Snyder, Sherry L. Snyder, John B. Stetson, Patty Stetson, Lynn Trusdell, John J. Twers, Jean Vicoli, and Richard Whiteford. I would also like to thank those individuals who wish to remain anonymous and James Nottage of the Gene Autry Museum. Mr. Nottage was very generous with his time and information. I only wish we could have met face to face.

Several public institutions opened their doors to me as well. I wish to extend my appreciation to the following organizations and their staffs: The Atwater Kent Museum, the Hagley Museum and Library, the Historical Society of Pennsylvania, the Pennsylvania State Archives, and the Temple University Business Archives.

Finally, I would also like to extend my appreciation to the many residents of Philadelphia and the surrounding region who had additional stories to tell and objects to show. I wish I could have visited you all.

Introduction

Mention Stetson hats and images of cowboys and adventure spring to mind — cowboys driving cattle up a dusty trail, cowboys "bustin' broncos," cowboys performing stunts in Buffalo Bill's Wild West Show, or cowboys singing and brawling on Hollywood's silver screen. John B. Stetson's famous "Boss of the Plains" cowboy hats, and all the high crowned, wide brimmed, soft felt western hats that followed, are intimately associated with the cowboy image. They were essential tools for anyone working in the intense heat or stinging cold of the open range. John Wayne christened them collectively "the hat that won the West."

A Boss of the Plains style western Stetson popular from the 1860s through the turn of the twentieth century. This hat was owned by the cowboy who wore the gloves decorated with the lone star. He must have been a Texan. The crown measures 4" high and the brim measures 3" wide. *Courtesy of the Peter C. Schubert collection.*

The cowboy in this tin type is completely outfitted, including his hat. *Courtesy of the Peter C. Schubert collection.*

Think of Stetson hats and images of cowboys leap to mind. Cowboys driving cattle, ... *Courtesy of John J. Twers.*

However, the dusty cowboy hat is only part of the story. Speaking generally, Stetson hats may be divided into two broad categories, western hats and dress hats. Cowboys and city slickers, cowgirls and grand dames all wore Stetsons produced at the John B. Stetson Company factory in Philadelphia, Pennsylvania, from c. 1870 to 1970.[1]

Stetson hats, both western and dress, came in all shapes and sizes. There was a Stetson for just about every occasion. From the 1870s onward, men had their choice of many hat styles, whether they rode the range or the trolley car every day. By the late 1800s, the company was making Stetson "outdoors hats" for women. In 1930, ladies dress hats adorned with netting, beads, and feathers were first produced.

In the decades following World War II, more and more Americans put their hats aside and went out into the world bareheaded. With steadily declining sales, the John B. Stetson Company closed the doors on its Philadelphia factory forever in 1971, licensing the Stetson name out to another American firm to continue the Stetson line.

... cowboys busting broncos, ... *Courtesy of John J. Twers.*

Stetson hats came in handy for driving sheep too. *Courtesy of John J. Twers.*

... and cowboys working in the corral. *Courtesy of John J. Twers.*

City slickers also wore Stetson hats. This hat is marked Royal Stetson, is made of olive colored felt hat with a wide hat band. It was sold by Strawbridge and Clothier and is of a style popular in the 1930s and 1940s. *Courtesy of Patty Stetson.* $125-200

This Stetson exudes cowboy character. Cowboys wore their Stetsons to death before ever thinking of giving them up or breaking in another hat. That makes early Stetsons difficult to find. This example is missing its sweatband. *Courtesy of Dick Engel.* $50-100 (in its well-worn condition)

In 1930 the Stetson Company began to manufacture women's millinery as well. This is a 1950s pink felt hat covered with silver glass beads, and salmon colored sequins and a veil. It is labeled Stetson, 1224 Chestnut Street, Philadelphia (the address of Stetson's local retail shop). *Courtesy of Desire Smith.* $65-85

Basic Definitions

When dealing with hats, it is comforting to know that while proportions, decorations, and scale change with the whims of fashion, basic hat style has changed little in the past five hundred years. There are only two basic hat styles, brimmed and unbrimmed, which come in two basic forms, hats and caps. These are most often produced in one of two materials, felt or straw.[2]

Felt is an unwoven fabric matted together by pressure. It is made from wool, fur, or hair. The Stetson Company made their felt from the fur of rabbits, beaver, muskrat, and coypu — a South American aquatic rodent introduced into both the Gulf Coast and the Pacific Northwest in the United States. Felt made from the fur of the coypu is called "nutria."[3]

There are specific terms for various portions of a hat's anatomy. The crown is the part of the hat rising above the brim or the shape on the hat's top. The crease is the shape of the crown, created by a series of dents on the top and/or sides of the crown. There are many crease shapes, some creases are associated with specific regions of the United States. Block can refer either to the shape of the crown or to a wooden die used to form that shape. Brim refers to the portion of the hat below the crown. Flange (and brim roll) names the shape of the brim or the die used to form that shape. The sweatband is an inner band sewn into the hat, usually made of leather—its purpose is self-evident in the name.[4]

There are also terms dealing with the appearance of the hat. The silhouette or profile is that combination of crown (crease/block) and brim (flange) that creates a hat's distinctive shape or silhouette. Scope is the brim's side view, presenting the front and back roll of the brim.[5]

All of the essential pieces of hat anatomy are visible in this fairly new Number 1 Quality Stetson with a 3 1/2" brim, and a 5 1/4" crown. A small cowboy pin and two feathers decorate the hat band. A well known Stetson image titled "The Last Drop From His Stetson" adorns the lining, showing a cowboy watering his horse from his hat. *Courtesy of Lynn Trusdell.* $200-300

This is the Boss of the Plains style which launched John B. Stetson toward hat making fame. *Courtesy of Dick Engel.*

Who Wore Stetson Hats?

"No cheap, apologetic, sneakerino tightwad ever wore a Stetson—it wouldn't fit him."

— Elbert Hubbard, 1911[6]

A city-slicker in a Stetson fedora let the world know he was doing well. British actor George Arliss is shown wearing his gray velour dress Stetson in the November 1925 issue of *The Hat Box*, a newsletter written by Stetson employees. *Courtesy of the author's collection.*

These are not hat wearing times. Back in the 1870s when John Batterson Stetson started selling his hats in earnest, it was a different story. Nobody went bareheaded and almost anybody could tell you something about a man's social status, attitudes, and beliefs or a woman's class, upbringing, and marital status by the hat perched on that person's head. Back then, wearing a Stetson spoke volumes. As Elbert Hubbard so subtly pointed out, these hats were expensive, high quality gear. From the moment Stetson started producing his trademark "Boss Of The Plains" western hat, he offered it at prices ranging from five to thirty dollars apiece depending on the quality of the felt involved. These were steep prices for the 1870s. The cowboy riding the range wearing that Boss of the Plains or the city-slicker in a Stetson fedora let the world know he was doing well.

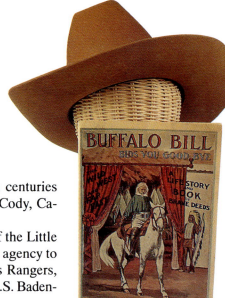

Colonel William F. Cody wore a Stetson. "Buffalo Bill Bids You Goodbye." The Farewell Salute and Official Review. February 2, 1910. *Courtesy of Lynn Trusdell.* $300-500

Familiar figures from the late nineteenth and early twentieth centuries who wore Stetsons included Colonel William F. ("Buffalo Bill") Cody, Calamity Jane, Will Rogers, and Annie Oakley.

Legend has it General George A. Custer rode into the Battle of the Little Big Horn wearing his Stetson. The first American law-enforcement agency to adopt Stetson's western hat as part of their uniform was the Texas Rangers, although many would follow. After the Boer War, British general R.S.S. Baden-Powell ordered 10,000 Stetsons. The future leader of the Boy Scouts gave them to the South African police force. The Royal Canadian Mounted Police, police forces in over thirty American states, members of the National Park Service, Border Patrol, Army and Air Force Drill and Rifle Teams, and the U.S. Marine Corps all followed suit, donning various Stetson styles.[7]

Many rodeo riders from Cheyenne and Calgary to Pendleton and Fort Worth wore Stetsons. Notable women starring in rodeos wore Stetsons as well. Ruth Roach, a favorite on the rodeo circuit from c. 1914-1927, wore a high crowned Stetson western hat. Faye Johnson Blesing was a headliner with the Madison Square Garden Championship Rodeo for seven years in the 1930s. Popular and beautiful, Blesing's endorsement was sought by many manufacturers, including Stetson. The Stetson Company created a western hat for her with a "Faye Blesing Crease." Blesing later went on to work in the movie industry as a stunt double.[8]

Actors were some of the most visible Stetson wearers, including Tom Mix, Douglas Fairbanks, Gene Autry, Roy Rogers, and Dale Evans. More recently, John Wayne, Burt Reynolds, Dennis Weaver, and James Coburn wore them.

Presidents Truman, Eisenhower, and Johnson all preferred to wear the Stetson "Open Road," a small, formal western Stetson. Officials of all sorts from mayors and presidents to princes and pontiffs have been given Stetson hats as gifts at one time or another. In 1981 it was reported that a ten gallon Stetson had been given to Pope John Paul II.

British general R.S.S. Baden-Powell ordered 10,000 Stetsons for the South African police. This style has been worn by military men, rangers, and state troopers alike for many years. No. 1 Quality stiff brimmed, raw edged hat with a 5 1/2" high crown and 3" wide brim. *Courtesy of Bruce Mackinnon.* $75-125

Stetson hats presented as gifts are highly prized collectibles. They carry a presentation label stamped into the leather of the sweatband which includes the name of the person receiving the hat. In a news photograph dated August 26, 1946, copies of such labels bearing the names of famous men were shown hanging on a wall of the Stetson printing department as trophies. The names of some of the notables on those presentation labels included Will Rogers, Winston Churchill, Fred Allen, and Franklin D. Roosevelt. The labels read either "Made by John B. Stetson Company Especially For ..." or "Made by Stetson Especially For ...".

Many actors have worn Stetsons over the years. Leading men preferred theirs to be large and white. Tom Mix not only wore this style, he carried eighteen of them with him when traveling internationally. These he gave to officials and dignitaries he met. *Courtesy of the author's collection.*

Women rodeo stars wore Stetsons as well. Ruth Roach wore one similar to this beautiful, early cowgirl's Stetson with a 7 1/2" brim and 8" crown. *Courtesy of Dick Engel.* $500-700

Gene Autry is shown with one of those big, white Stetsons in this Gene Autry Show Souvenir Program from 1950. *Courtesy of Lynn Trusdell.* $75-100

Here Gene is selling wallets for Sears in the Fall and Winter of 1942. © 1942-43, Sears, Roebuck and Co.

12

"The King of Jazz," band leader Paul Whiteman proudly wears the Stetson that was made especially for him. He began his radio career in 1922 and was one of the pioneers of television. These are his personal tooled holster and gauntlets, as seen in the photograph. *Courtesy of Lynn Trusdell.*

Roy wore them too! Roy Rogers comic book dated January 1951. *Courtesy of Lynn Trusdell.* $100-125

A favorite among presidents Truman, Eisenhower, and Johnson was the Open Road. This example has a 4" high crown and a 2 1/2" wide brim. *Courtesy of W.D. Clarke.* $75-100

Stetson hat box addressed to Mayor Richardson Dilworth, Room 202 City Hall. *Courtesy of The Atwater Kent Museum.* NP

Philadelphia mayor Richardson Dilworth's, who visited the Stetson factory from time to time, wore this dapper, gray homburg (a homburg has a center creased crown and the curled brim you see here). According to the label, Wanamaker's sold this hat to the mayor. Mr. Dilworth had entered politics in the 1930s and served as mayor from January 1956 to February 1962. *Courtesy of The Atwater Kent Museum.* NP (**N**o **P**rice will be given for museum pieces.)

Another example of a Stetson given as a gift. Lewis Nelson, a famous Wyoming ranch cook, received this western hat on his birthday in 1925 as a token of appreciation from "The Eastern Dudes" who vacationed at Shoshone Forest Wyoming Ranch. The hat was purchased in Cody. Mr. Nelson appears a bit puzzled by the hat. *Courtesy of the author's collection.*

Stetsons were given as retirement gifts by the company. This impressive gray fedora (a hat with center and side creases in the crown and a wide, flexible brim) was given to John Latzko "upon retirement after years of faithful service." This hat was made of very fine "Stetson Clear Beaver Quality" felt. *Courtesy of John J. Twers.* $200-300 (for the hat)

Like Lewis Nelson, W.H. Russell was also the recipient of an impressive Stetson clear nutria felt western hat. Cut into the sweatband is the inscription: "Compliments of the Round-Up to W.H. Russell. Pendleton, Ore. 1914." The sweatband was also marked "The Fray" and with the Stetson Company "Clear Nutria" mark. Nutria fur was considered to make a very high quality felt. This hat measures 7" high at the crown and 5" wide at the brim. *Courtesy of the collection of Charlie and Karla Smith.* $1200-1400

The World's Most Expensive Hat

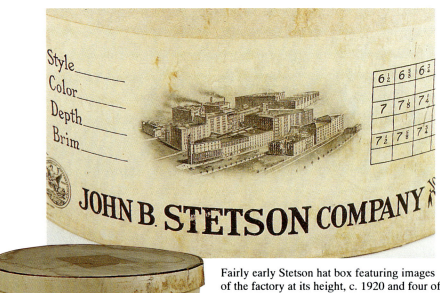

Fairly early Stetson hat box featuring images of the factory at its height, c. 1920 and four of the quality marks found stamped in sweatbands. The average oval hat box measures 13" x 14 1/2" wide oval, standing 7" high. Boxes capable of holding two hats measures approximately 13 3/4" high. *Courtesy of Patty Stetson*. The more elaborate the decoration or the rarer the box, the higher the price will be. Hat boxes range in value from $25-75.

A labor intensive western Stetson, claimed by the company to be the world's most expensive hat, was created in 1955. Forty-three workers spent a year assembling a western hat worth $1,500 at that time. It was made of beaver felt, had a 3 1/2" brim, and was trimmed with a sterling silver band in the shape of a double rope strand. A solid gold longhorn steer head was added for ornamentation. This creation toured Australia, Columbia, Germany, Mexico, New Zealand, and Tokyo. Collectors all over the globe must be wondering where that hat is today.[9]

Amazing Claims of Strength

Stetsons were as durable as they were expensive. For cowboys, Stetsons were a major investment and they wore their hats for years on end. Even when the hats were finally in tatters, their owners were reluctant to part with them. This is one reason collecting old Stetson western hats can be a challenge.

Even so, in 1924 and 1927 the Stetson company reported two cases of hat durability which strain the limits of belief. In the first, on February 28, 1924 a road crew in Weeksville, Montana, uncovered the grave of two bandits dating from 1882. Vigilantes working with the Northern Pacific Railroad had caught them, strung them up, and buried them with their boots on ... and their Stetsons. While "Ohio Jim" and his luckless partner were in pretty bad shape, their Stetsons "were still in good condition. The felt showed little sign of corrosion and the Stetson imprint was easily read."[10]

The second story returns a hat from a watery grave:

"A striking illustration of the durability of a Stetson hat is the fact that in 1912, when the hulk of the battleship Maine, which had been sunk in Havana harbor in 1898, was raised and explored, one of the objects found aboard was a Stetson hat. This had been submerged in sea-water for 14 years; it had been exposed to the action of ooze, mud, and sea-growths of the waters of the harbor. And yet it was still capable of being renovated; in fact, it was renovated and to all appearances was as good as ever."[11]

That is one durable hat!

Keep your eyes open. You never know where the next tough old Stetson hat will turn up.

"Hat's Not All Folks!" Other Collectibles from the John B. Stetson Company

While this book focuses on the hats produced by John Batterson Stetson and his company from 1865 to 1970, there are many other items associated with the company which are worthy of a collector's notice. Hat boxes are among the most obvious of these. They come in many shapes and sizes. Hat boxes were made at the Stetson factory and held one or several hats. Cardboard rings and stays supported the hats within the box. Studying old photographs and company advertisements will help determine the age of specific hat box styles.

A load of 4000 boxed Stetsons are delivered to the company's Philadelphia retail shop in 1925. *Courtesy of the author's collection.*

A more recent hat box capable of holding two hats. *Courtesy of Patty Stetson.*

Hat boxes capable of holding several straw hats being packed at the Stetson factory in 1922. *Courtesy of the Pennsylvania State Archives.*

Cardboard rings and stays supported the hats within the box. This box bears the paper Stetson Hat Shop, 1224 Chestnut Street, Philadelphia 7 PA label. *Courtesy of Desire Smith.*

Old photographs can help to determine the approximate age of particular hat box styles. This photo was published in 1965. *Courtesy of Irene Centofanti.*

The hat box appearing in the 1965 photograph. *Courtesy of the author's collection.*

The Stetson Company manufactured their own hat boxes within the factory's walls. *Courtesy of Desire Smith.*

Another example of the square shape hat box. *Courtesy of the author's collection.*

Oval tan Stetson hat box bearing the Philadelphia retail shop address, 1224 Chestnut Street. It is decorated with city scapes of major cities where Stetson retail shops and offices could be found — New York, Philadelphia, London, and Paris. London and Paris offices opened in the early 1920s. *Courtesy of The Atwater Kent Museum.*

Hat boxes with adjustable leather straps to keep the lids closed. *Black and brown boxes courtesy of Patty Stetson. The green box is courtesy of Jean Vicoli.*

Hat boxes featuring historic landmarks in Stetson's home town of Philadelphia in two different coloring motifs. *Courtesy of Patty Stetson and Lynn Trusdell.*

Hat box with nostalgic city motifs, no doubt protecting a Stetson dress hat and not a western style.
Courtesy of Patty Stetson.

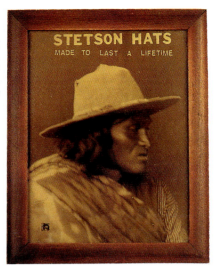

Stetson advertisement featuring Do Gow. The photo was taken by Karl Moon. The poster reads, "Stetson Hats. Made to Last a Lifetime." *Courtesy of Jack Laura.*

Interior of a modern Stetson western featuring the image "The Last Drop From His Stetson" on the lining. This is the single most famous advertisement the company produced. *Courtesy of Richard Whiteford.*

Advertising art and posters are available. Window cards were produced for a new year's advertising campaign and displayed in shops carrying Stetson hats early in the twentieth century. In 1924, the new cards included four cut out cards showing the downtown business districts of cities which were the "style centers of the country," including New York, Philadelphia, and Los Angeles. Other window cards displayed a particular hat on a model. One memorable card shows a beaver standing on a hillside with a tree in the upper right corner and bears the phrase "STETSON 3X BEAVER QUALITY FIFTEEN DOLLARS AND UP."[12]

The single most famous advertising poster the company ever produced was titled "The Last Drop From His Stetson" in which a cowboy is shown watering his horse from his hat. This image continues to be used in the lining inside Stetson hats today.

Other paper products of interest include Stetson stock certificates, company letter head, and books or pamphlets produced by the company. A company booklet containing news about the company and its employees and created by them called *The Hat Box* makes fascinating reading. Look for examples of paper products in good condition, free of stains or tears.

Many paper products associated with the company are available to collectors. *Courtesy of Irene Centofanti.* Collectibles related to the Stetson Company add interesting accents to any collection and are very valuable sources of information; however, these items tend not to be very valuable in monetary terms, generally ranging from $25-40 on average. Of course, unusual or unique items will be worth more, at times substantially more.

A copy of Elbert Hubbard's 1911 book about the life and times of John B. Stetson. *Courtesy of Patty Stetson.*

A letter to the stockholders on company letterhead dating from 1963. *Courtesy of Patty Stetson.*

A copy of the May 1925 edition of *The Hat Box*, featuring Tom Mix on the cover. These booklets are filled with news about Stetson employees and the company's products. *Courtesy of the author's collection.*

Many find the company's wooden hat blocks to be very collectible. A Stetson label is found on this block. *Courtesy of The Atwater Kent Museum.*

Hat flanges were made of cherry wood. *Courtesy of Patty Stetson.*

From within the Stetson factory itself, many find the wooden blocks and flanges to be highly collectible. Poplar wood blocks were used to shape and finish the hats and cherry wood flanges curled the brims of felt and straw hats alike. Of particular interest are the special blocks which were made specifically for famous individuals and were marked with their names. Hats shaped on one of these special blocks were only made for the individual named on that block. Many of the early Western stars had their own Stetson blocks, including Tom Mix.

Blocks and flanges could only be used if they remained in perfect condition. Once they were chipped, they were discarded. Today's John B. Stetson, the grand nephew of the firm's founder, states that many of these discarded blocks suffered a singular fate. His father, Willis George Stetson, was in charge of the company's specialty hats for many years. When hat blocks were damaged and were no longer useful, Willis Stetson would bring them home in the trunk of his car and his son John would chop them into fire wood. John Stetson remembers that the blocks he chopped burned well but he does not recall if any of the blocks he consigned to the wood pile had names on them.[13]

John B. Stetson, the company founder, began giving company Christmas parties in the nineteenth century and the tradition outlived him, continuing until 1930. During these parties, gifts were given by the company to employees and their families. Among these gifts were gloves and candy for the ladies, hats and inscribed pocket watches with chains for the gentlemen. Surely, some of these items are still in circulation.

The hat size, 7 1/8, and crown height, 5 3/4, are stamped into the base of this block. *Courtesy of Patty Stetson.*

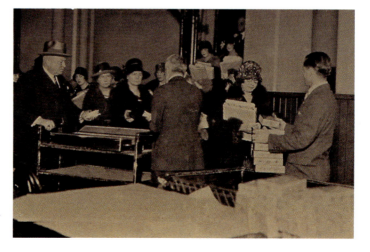

Ladies receive boxes of candy at the Stetson Christmas party. *Courtesy of the author's collection.*

Christmas gift miniature hat box. *Courtesy of Peggy A. DeAngelo.* $50-75

Miniature Stetson hats and hat boxes are associated with gift-giving as well. A customer could go into a Stetson retail shop and order a hat for a friend or loved one without knowing the size of the recipients head. Small hat boxes containing miniature hats were kept in the store to assist such customers. Different styles of tiny hats and hat boxes indicated full sized hats in different price ranges (and presumably of different hat styles). When the customer chose a hat of a particular quality, that customer received a miniature hat box and hat that represented full-sized hats in that price range. The person presented with the miniature hat box would bring it back to the retail shop and a clerk would direct him or her to the hats in the price range indicated by that particular tiny hat box.

Additional items associated with the John B. Stetson Company will be discussed throughout the book. During the final decades, this Philadelphia firm diversified its product lines to include shirts, shoes, neck ties, and other articles of apparel, all of which carry the Stetson name.

A full-sized Stetson hat box and its miniature counterpart in a Christmas motif. These were for the gift-giver who was not sure of the birthday boy's hat size. *Courtesy of Desire Smith and Peggy A. DeAngelo.* $50-75 for miniature boxes without hats.

This miniature box not only had the molded plastic hat, but a miniature felt hat in the 1940s dress hat style that fit over it perfectly. *Courtesy of Patty Stetson.* $100-125

This miniature box has a plastic molded snap brim hat. *Courtesy of John J. Twers.* Miniature boxes with their miniature hats are worth $100-125

Another miniature box decorated in a Christmas motif, containing an identical 1940s style molded plastic hat. *Courtesy of Patty Stetson.* $100-125

Yet another miniature Christmas hat box with a plastic hat molded in the small snap brim style popular among city-folk in the 1950s. *Courtesy of The Atwater Kent Museum.* NP

An extraordinarily detailed miniature hat came with this box. It appears to be a brown felt derby; the details (the ventilation holes and trim) are not usually seen. The hat measures 3" in diameter and 1 1/2" high. The box is 4 1/4" x 3 5/8" x 2 3/4" high. *Courtesy of Desire Smith.* $100-175 for this unique item.

As you can see, miniature hat boxes with a wide range of Christmas motifs were produced. *Courtesy of Patty Stetson.* $50-75

Blocky little black hats came with these miniature boxes. *Courtesy of Patty Stetson.* $100-125

Western hats also had their miniature counterparts. *Courtesy of Patty Stetson.* $100-125

The Stetson name has become synonymous with the wide-brimmed, soft felt hat with a tall crown worn in the American West by men riding the open range. A wonderful dark blue clear nutria felt staple hat that fits the image, labeled "John B. Stetson Co. Phila. Waterproof." *Courtesy of The Atwater Kent Museum.* NP

A staple hat in a style similar to one identified as the Baden-Powell in Stetson's 1901 catalog. The No. 1 Quality mark in the sweatband was used specifically on soft staple hats. The merchant's name and Glacier Park, Montana, address are also found printed on the sweatband. *Courtesy of Elmer and Jan Diederich.* $75-125

Chapter I

Stetson Hats and Their Methods of Manufacture

In the minds of many, the name Stetson is a generic term for a wide-brimmed, soft felt hat with a tall crown worn in the American West by men on the open range. In reality, the range of Stetson hats produced is much broader. There are staple and dress hats, stiff and conforming hats, hats made of different qualities of felt, hats of straw, hats with finished brims and raw edged brims, and kettle finished hats which never lose their curl.

In this chapter, early Stetson catalogs from 1899 and 1901 are used to explain the broad categories the Stetson Company used to identify their hats. A brief step-by-step description of felt hat manufacturing follows to further illustrate the way Stetsons were assembled. Changing hat styles will be covered in Chapters III and IV.

Staple and Dress Hats

There are two broad categories into which all Stetson hats fall, the staple hats and the dress hats. The staple hats are the western hats. They are also called soft hats, stockmen's hats, or cowboy hats. While there have been

Examples of Stetson produced women's dress hats manufactured in straw. Both are labeled "Stetson 5th Avenue" and "Claire Hat Shop/ Pottstown PA". *Courtesy of Desire Smith*. $60-75 each

many staple hat shapes made over the years, identified with colorful names such as Boss of the Plains, Austin, Baden Powell, and Lincoln, these hats do not change their shapes nearly as often as the dress hats. In 1901 staple hats were offered in the following colors: black, blue-black, otter belly, side and back nutria. The last three were natural fur colors. In 1940, the biggest change in staple hats in many years was the introduction of pastel colors for movie cowboys and rodeo riders.[1]

Dress hat was the catchall term for every other style of Stetson hat. These were also called town hats. There were many dress hat styles produced over the years including bowlers, homburgs, fedoras, trilbys or snap brims, and straw panamas, telescopes, and boaters. Also remember that both of these broad categories include women's hats as well. Once John B. Stetson established his business with the staple hats, he entered the dress hat market to keep a balance to his business and to ensure future growth.

"Imperial" Stetson straw boater marked "John B. Stetson Company Fifth Avenue, New York". The flat crowned, broad brimmed straw boater, with its wide hat band, was a popular hat during the early decades of the twentieth century. Men worn boaters for leisurely summer outings including boating (of course) or seaside visits. *Courtesy of Patty Stetson*. $50-75

There were many dress hat styles, including the homburg shown here. This homburg is listed as a "Royal De Luxe" Stetson. The merchant and his New Jersey shop location, "Konner's Patterson", are printed in gold on the sweatband. Named for the German town where it originated, the homburg had a high, creased crown and a narrow, curved brim. This was a popular soft felt hat through the 1940s. Edward, the Prince of Wales (b. 1841 - d. 1910 [Edward VII, King of England, 1901-1910]) brought the homburg to broad public attention and popularity in England. *Courtesy of John J. Twers*. $75-125

Stiff Hats

At the turn of the twentieth century, under the broad category of dress hats there were several interesting distinctions among hat styles. Stiff hats (bowlers [a.k.a. derbies] and fedoras) were not flexible, they had been given a coat of shellac during their construction to stiffen them and they did not conform to the shape of the wearer's head. This was a problem for individuals with the lumpy heads Victorian phrenologists loved to study. Stiff hats included the Stetson Special, Stetson Style, and the Philadelphia Style.

Bowlers—long the symbol of masculine power dressing—were divided into stiff hats, self-conforming, and flexible hats. The height of the stiff bowler's crown varied from 4 1/2" to 5 3/4" and 6" deep. The brims ranged from 1 5/8" to 2 1/4" and 2 1/2" in width.

The self-conforming and flexible bowlers had more give to them. They shaped themselves to fit the heads they were placed on. These were more comfortable to wear. Among the stiff, self-conforming, and flexible bowlers were lighter weight models termed "Featherweight."[2]

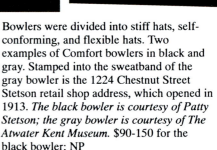

The Flexible Conforming stamp indicates this bowler is not stiff and will shape itself to the wearer's head for a more comfortable fit. *Courtesy of Elmer and Jan Diederich.*

Bowlers were divided into stiff hats, self-conforming, and flexible hats. Two examples of Comfort bowlers in black and gray. Stamped into the sweatband of the gray bowler is the 1224 Chestnut Street Stetson retail shop address, which opened in 1913. *The black bowler is courtesy of Patty Stetson; the gray bowler is courtesy of The Atwater Kent Museum.* $90-150 for the black bowler; NP

Novelty Hats

Novelty hats is a catchall term for a variety of stylish shapes designed to be worn while playing golf and other outdoor sports. Many early novelty hats had a deep central crease in the crown and a variety of creases along the side of the crowns. They also had upturned brims and decorative hatbands varying from narrow to wide. The most popular novelty hat colors were the natural shades: Natural Russia, Belly, and Side Nutria. Names of novelty hats included Golf, Bob White, Nugget, and Tuxedo.[3] Later novelty hats had telescope crowns.

Hat Brims

Generally speaking, hat brims were produced both in flat shapes and curled. An example of a flat brimmed is the Boss of the Plains western (or staple) hat. Curled hat brims were called "Flange Brims" or "Tourist styles." The flange from which this brim takes its name was a cherry wood form upon which the brim was placed to be curled.[4]

A more recent 4X Beaver felt western hat in the short, stockman style with a curled brim. It has a lining adorned with "The Last Drop From His Stetson." The crown measures 4 1/2" high; the brim measures 2 3/4" wide. *Courtesy of W.D. Clarke.* $125-200

A Boss of the Plains style western Stetson with a flat brim. The sweatband is marked, "Cananea Consolidated Copper Company Mercantile Department. The gauntleted gloves are an interesting addition. They are of American Indian origin and are made of buffalo hide. *Courtesy of the Peter C. Schubert collection.* $150-250 hat; $500-650 gloves.

An example of the pencil rolled brim on a white No. 1 Quality staple hat. There is no silk lining. 6" high crown, 3 1/2" wide brim. *Courtesy of Ray Huffman, Broken Heart Trading.* $300-400

A bound edge has a strip of material sewn over the outer edge of the hat brim. This style was popular in the 1920s and before. This is a No. 1 Quality fur hat sold by "Connolly Bros. Makers of the Original Connolly Saddle. Billings, Mont." The crown measures 7 1/2" high and the brim 5" wide. *Courtesy of the collection of Charlie and Karla Smith.* $500-700

One of the three binding techniques is well illustrated on this Stetson — the binding is predominantly along the outer edge of the brim. This particular hat was sold by the Cody Trading Company of Cody, Wyoming. It has a 7 1/2" high crown and a 5 1/2" wide brim. *Courtesy of the collection of Larry and Marylin Robinson.* $600-800

Depending on the method used to produce the hat, hat brims could have a bound, welted, or a "raw" edge. Also, the edge could be folded, or "pencil rolled." In that case, an oversized edge is doubled back and turned into the crown. Once this was pressed and ironed, it formed a soft, rounded edge and a double brim.

A bound edge has a thin strip of material (binding) sewn over the outer edge of the hat brim. This binding finished the edge and helped maintain the brim's shape, holding the curl, or "snap." The binding was also decorative. Binding color and width could effect the overall look of the hat. A wide binding made the brim look narrower than it was and was an added expense. Narrow bindings made brims look wider. Lighter colored bindings made dark hats look lighter and vice versa.

There were three kinds of binding: bindings which were the same width on the top and bottom of the brim, bindings which were narrower on the top brim, and bindings which were narrower on the bottom brim. Various stitching styles were employed to fasten the binding to the brim. The regular or through stitch is visible on both sides of the brim. The concealed stitch showed no stitching on the outside of the rolled brim and was used on homburgs. There were also ornamental stitches such as the saddle stitch. Finally there was the hand-sewn binding. Hand-sewn bindings were extremely labor intensive and time consuming and are not often seen.[5]

The welt edge was a different method for strengthening the brim and reducing the chance of damage through daily handling. The welt edge was a brim edge folded back upon itself, either over or under, and attached. There are different types of welts but they are formed using similar processes. The hat brim was curled, a properly sized zinc plate was laid on the brim and the curled edge was turned back and ironed flat over the upper surface of the plate. At that point the welt was stitched down and excess fur was cut away.[6]

Using a different manufacturing process, the less costly "boss raw edge" required no binding around the outer edge of the brim to maintain its shape and keep a clean, unraveled edge. For a finishing touch the raw edge could be slanted or rounded, lending additional strength to the brim.[7]

Finishes

There are several ways to finish a hat, each of which adds to its look and name. The most eye-catching is the silk finish, a long fur finish with a silky sheen. The angora finish is similar in look and feel to the silk, and refers to the furry look and feel of the finish, not to any use of angora itself. The beaver finish has a long nap that is combed back horizontally. It does not refer to the amount of beaver fur in the felt itself. Velour finish is renown for a deep, lustrous nap similar to fine velvet and is the most pleasant finish to touch. Suede finish is also known as an antelope or doe finish. It has a slight sheen, differentiating it from a regular smooth-finish felt and is soft and velvety to the touch. A sponge, chinchilla, or pebble finish has many tiny knobs or clumps of fur covering the surface of the hat, creating a nubby look. Finally, the scratch finish is created by scratching the fur surface with a wire brush in the last stages of manufacture. Any type of felt may be used, leaving the surface hairs either rough and hairy or laid into a long, smooth nap with additional brushing.[8]

Boss Raw Edge Kettle Finish

This is a Stetson hand finishing technique. Hats made of nutria or beaver felt were curled and shaped at the kettle, applying hot water to the brim and carefully curling it. This process created a hat that would retain its shape under extreme weather conditions. No binding was needed to keep the curl in the brim. Kettle finished brims ranged from heavily to slightly curled. Style names of hats finished in this way included Richmond, Sorento, panama, Graeco, Express, Niagara, Columbia, Denver, Dakota, and Buffalo Bill.[9]

Hat Linings

Quality hat linings were first made of fine satins. Later synthetic linings of rayon were produced, either satin or taffeta rayon. Taffeta rayon is lighter weight and is used in lighter weight hats. To keep linings in place, they are sewn in at the base of the brim and tailored to fit the inside of the hat exactly. The better the skill of the craftsman, the better the lining would fit.

In the best quality hats, different linings were made for each head size to create an exact fit. Lesser hats could use linings for different crown heights provided that they did not vary by more than 1/4 inch. The sweatband would hide any discrepancy in the fit.[10]

Purple lining in a 1920s style western hat. *Courtesy of the collection of Charlie and Karla Smith.*

Why is this bow here? Courtesy of the author's collection.

Exactly what *is* that little bow at the back of the sweatband for? Explanations are wide ranging and include: the bow is a holdover from an earlier age when such a string adjusted one-size-fits-all hats to the wearer's head, or that the bow is either a gentle reminder to the wearer as to where the back of the hat is supposed to be or a simple hatter's measure, locating the center of the back of the hat. The most intriguing idea is that the bow is a stylized skull and crossbones danger symbol used in days-gone-by to remind wearers that toxic mercury had been used in the felting process (a problem which sickened many hatters but was remedied later with better ventilation and the substitution of other chemicals for mercury). The bow and sizing label found in this Stetson Open Road are very suggestive of the latter explanation.

Hatbands

Hatbands encircle the crown just above the brim. Early hatbands were adjustable leather belts used to adjust the hat's fit. Decorative hatbands were made of woven silver or gold wire. A rattlesnake skin sometimes replaced the leather band. Later bands were made of silk and were merely decorative.[11]

Hatbands encircle the crown just above the brim. Courtesy of Elmer and Jan Diederich. $300-400

Hat Qualities, Trademarks, and Labels

The Stetson Company used the fur from American and Canadian beaver and muskrat, "nutria" from the Argentine coypu, and fur from the hare from Continental Europe and the Scottish and English coney (a European rabbit) to make their felt. The best quality fur from the beaver, muskrat, and coypu was the belly fur; from the hares and coneys the back fur was best. The higher the quality of the fur used to make the felt, the more expensive the hat made from that felt would be. According to the early catalogs, the quality of the felt and the size of the brim were the prime considerations in pricing Stetson hats.[12]

Hats using felt made of nutria or beaver were prominently noted among the Stetson trademarks as these were the highest quality felts. Trademarks were stamped into the sweatbands inside Stetson hats in either gold or silver. Trademarks for felt hats were often accompanied by "X" notations such as "1 X", "3 X", or "XXX" which indicated the density of the material. In essence, these were quality ratings, the more X's, the higher the quality of the felt. This "X rating" system ranged in grade from as low at 1X to as high as 10X. Hats made of material rated below 5X generally contained a poorer grade of fur with little or no beaver fur. A 10X hat contained 100% beaver fur. In years past this X rating system was a convenient rough pricing guide, as a 3X hat would cost $30, a 4X hat, $40, and so on. In the mid-1940s, a 10X Stetson cost $100 and was the finest hat available. Hats marked by Stetson with the phrase "Clear Beaver" were also of the highest quality, manufactured from pure, undyed beaver fur. A similar grading system was used in straw hats, replacing the X's with stars.[13]

Felt hats were accompanied with "X" notations which were quality ratings. As the quality of the felt increased, more X's were printed on the sweatbands. *Courtesy of James J. Snyder and Patty Stetson.*

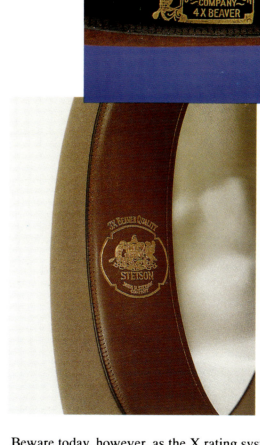

Beware today, however, as the X rating system no longer has the meaning it used to. The rating has become subjective as manufacturers and dealers have chosen to rate their hats differently, each following their own criteria, and they are using the X's as a price plateau instead of an actual quality rating system. Today's X rating system sets prices roughly like this: a 2X beaver is priced below $100, a 10X beaver at roughly $250; a 30X at $450, and a 100X beaver will set you back over $1000 to buy.[14]

As the X ratings vary by company, quiz Stetson dealers and distributors —or any other company you choose to purchase a hat from— to make sure you understand how they are using their X's. As a rule of thumb, a high quality felt hat should feel smooth and silky.[15]

Different trademarks were used to signify different types or qualities of hats. Some of these marks continued in use for many years.[16]

All of the following trademarks were in common use at the turn of the twentieth century and many continued to be used throughout the life of the company. This mark was used in hats requiring waterproofing which were made of real nutria and beaver quality felts. *Artwork courtesy of Gregory S. Ng.*

The trademark used in specially ordered soft or stiff hats. *Artwork courtesy of Gregory S. Ng.*

Trademark used only for the finest quality felt hats. *Artwork courtesy of Gregory S. Ng.*

As might be assumed, this trademark was used on 3X beaver grade hats. *Artwork courtesy of Gregory S. Ng.*

Used for flange brims and novelty hats. *Artwork courtesy of Gregory S. Ng.*

Used for staple soft hats of No. 1 quality (a grade not precisely defined in the literature this author has found to date). *Artwork courtesy of Gregory S. Ng.*

Used for staple soft hats of 1X nutria grade felts. *Artwork courtesy of Gregory S. Ng.*

Used in soft hats of nutria quality. *Artwork courtesy of Gregory S. Ng.*

A printed example of the No. 1 Quality trademark for soft staple hats. *Courtesy of Cowboy Trader Gallery.*

Used exclusively on Boss of the Plains style hats. *Artwork courtesy of Gregory S. Ng.*

Used in soft hats of real nutria quality. *Artwork courtesy of Gregory S. Ng.*

Used in flange brims and novelties, reveling in the company's grand prize award for the hats they displayed at the Paris Exhibition of 1900 (discussed in Chapter II). *Artwork courtesy of Gregory S. Ng.*

Used in stiff hats. *Artwork courtesy of Gregory S. Ng.*

Used in flexible stiff hats. *Artwork courtesy of Gregory S. Ng.*

Used in stiff hats. *Artwork courtesy of Gregory S. Ng.*

As discussed earlier, this trademark was used in self-conforming stiff hats. *Artwork courtesy of Gregory S. Ng.*

Used for stiff hats of premier and nutria quality. *Artwork courtesy of Gregory S. Ng.*

Stetson offered to print the marks of retailers onto the sweatbands of hats sold in their stores. These can be valuable hat dating tools if you can discover the years of operation of that particular shop.

Stetson offered to print the marks of retailers onto the sweatbands of hats to be sold in their stores. This is a rare Pendleton Roundup retailer's mark. *Courtesy of Dick Engel.*

The trademark used on clear nutria felt boss raw edge brimmed hats (brims which do not require binding along the edge). *Courtesy of Elmer and Jan Diederich.*

Stetson was not shy about printing the names of their own retail outlets into their sweatbands either. *Courtesy of Patty Stetson.*

Jack Reeds' Sons, Philadelphia shop printed in gold. *Courtesy of John J. Twers.*

Many fashionable retailer's preferred to have two labels in their hats, their own and the label with the manufacturer's name. Emme was a big name in women's fashions. *Courtesy of Desire Smith.*

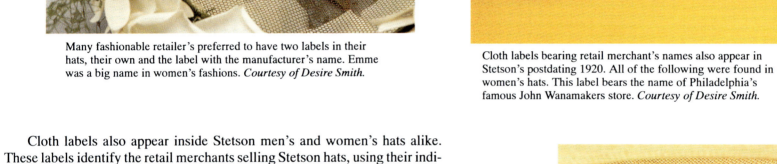

Cloth labels bearing retail merchant's names also appear in Stetson's postdating 1920. All of the following were found in women's hats. This label bears the name of Philadelphia's famous John Wanamakers store. *Courtesy of Desire Smith.*

Cloth labels also appear inside Stetson men's and women's hats alike. These labels identify the retail merchants selling Stetson hats, using their individual trademarks. Labels rarely appear in garments predating 1920.[17] A label can also be helpful in dating the hat in which it is found, provided you know the years the merchant listed on the label was in business. However, dating should never be based on the strength of the label alone.

A variety of cloth labels produced for Stetson's own shops in New York and Philadelphia in the 1950s. *Courtesy of Desire Smith.*

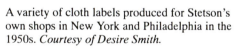

Manufacturing Felt Hats

Hats made of fur have many advantages over hats of other materials. Fur hats are lighter, they maintain their shape, and withstand weather and renovation better than most. To provide a clearer understanding of the Stetson felt hat, a brief description of the steps involved in its manufacture has been provided. Hat manufacturing techniques were developed and refined in the fourteenth century and have not changed substantially since, despite the introduction of more sophisticated technologies. The most basic steps involved in making a felt hat include bowing to remove and separate fur, basoning to firm the fur under pressure, and blocking to form the newly made felt into a hat.[18]

In 1922, the Stetson Company presented the Philadelphia school system with a book entitled *Hat Manufacture in Philadelphia*. While a little out of date, it still presents a detailed look at the basics of felt hat manufacture. Each step was completed within the sprawling nine acre Stetson factory complex. While new equipment improved the felt manufacturing and assembling processes, finishing and trimming was left to workers hands alone—workers who had completed "... long and severe apprenticeship[s]."[19]

Chemical Treatment

The first processing of the skins arriving at the factory was called "carrotting." A nitrate of mercury solution was brushed onto the fur, matting the fur, opening the scales on each fiber. The furs were then shrunk in hot water, interlocking the opened scales. Carrotting prepared the fur for felting.

Once shrunk, the furs could be allowed to dry naturally. Naturally dried furs were called "white carrotted." The furs could also be dried in an oven. Oven dried furs were referred to as "yellow carrotted" since the heat gave the furs a distinctive yellow cast.

Carrotted skins were taken to fur cellars for storage. Aging the furs was said to improve their quality. Depending on demand, furs could remain in the cellars for months.

Carroting the fur skins. Unless otherwise noted, these historical photographs (showing stages in the hat assembly process) from within the Stetson Company factory were taken from the 1922 volume *Hat Manufacture in Philadelphia*.

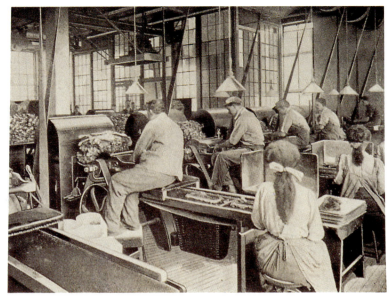
Removing fur from the hides.

Graded and packaged fur stacked in fur storerooms in the Stetson factory cellars.

Removing Fur from Hides

Furs recovered from the cellars was taken to the fur cutting department where they were first thoroughly brushed by machines, ensuring all the fibers would lie in one direction. Brushed furs were fed into another machine, separating fur from hide and cutting the hide into short shreds "... resembling shredded wheat...". Shredded hides were sold and made into glue.

In 1922, the Stetson Company used roughly twelve million fur skins, producing eight hundred and fifty thousand pounds of cut fur.

Sorting Fur for Grade and Color

Women sorted the cut fur by grade and color. Belly fur from aquatic animals was of the highest quality as was back fur from hares and coneys. Graded fur was packaged in five-pound paper bags and stacked in fur storerooms.

Blowing, Mixing, and Cleaning Fur

Moving on to the blowing department, fur was automatically fed into machines containing rotating cylinders studded with steel teeth called "pickers." The pickers tore the fibers apart. The torn fibers were then blown upward through several chambers, the unwanted, coarse, heavier outer hairs and debris falling away from the desired, lighter undercoat fur as it rose. Fur was blown several times to eliminate all unwanted materials. The processed furs were then mechanically blended to create the varying grades of felt used in the factory.

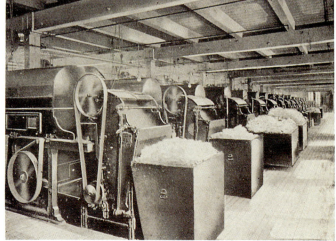
Machinery at work in the fur blowing department.

The Primary Felt Hat Form

This is the first stage in forming a felt hat body. At one end of a forming machine, blended fur is weighed to obtain the amount necessary to create a particular type of hat. Once weighed, the blended fur is fed into the machine where it is propelled into a chamber containing a revolving, perforated copper cone approximately three feet high. The turning cone pulls the mist-like fur particles down against its damp outer surface with suction. This forms a thin felt covering over the cone. Cone and felt are protected by flannel wrappings and a metal covering and placed in hot water. Once the felt is completely soaked, the resulting formed body is gently removed from the cone.

The new felt body is extremely delicate and must be kneaded by hard rubber rings in another machine to knit the fur fibers more tightly together. This produces a felt body durable enough to withstand subsequent processing.

Systematic Shrinking

The felt bodies were systematically shrunk in sets of three to their appropriate hat sizes. The bodies were thoroughly saturated with water, rolled in cloth, and immersed in hot water. The process is repeated until the bodies have shrunk by a third, the bodies unrolled and refolded in different ways with each immersion.

After the immersions are completed, hat bodies are worked individually, folded and pressed repeatedly to complete the process. The trick is to distribute the ever shrinking fur properly throughout the body, leaving the fur thinnest at the tip of the crown and thickest down at the brim.

Using machines to form the felt hat bodies. Note the three foot tall perforated copper cones in the foreground.

In this photograph of the sizing department, hat blocks are clearly visible in the rack in the foreground. Felt hat bodies in several styles are also visible. *Courtesy of the Pennsylvania State Archives.*

Sizing hat bodies, one of the hottest, wettest, least pleasant jobs in the plant. Workers stand on platforms in an attempt to keep their shoes dry. The author overheard two men discussing the one and only time they sought employment at Stetson decades ago. They were to be started in the sizing department. As soon as they walked into the room, both decided to seek employment elsewhere.

Dyeing

Hat bodies which were not to retain their natural fur coloring were sent on to the coloring department where they were given dye-baths. Different combinations of anthracene or alizarine dyes were used depending on the mixtures of fur in the hat body. Stiff hats remained in the baths for over two hours while soft hats soaked for about three, after which they were all rinsed and dried. The colored bodies were now ready for the stiffening department.

Shaping the Conical Felt Body

In the pulling-out department, the hat body is once again sunk in boiling water. Into another machine the boiled body goes, where it is stretched over a metal "skeleton block." The crown is pulled out or flattened. Another machine pulls out the brim and the body begins to take on a familiar hat shape.

At this point, the pulled or flattened body is sent on to the blocking department. Once again, the body was worked in hot water, this time on a wooden block. The shape and size of the completed hat was set at this time. The brim was pulled and stretched until it was absolutely flat, sharply angled from the crown. The hat was then dipped in cold water, removed from the wooden block, and dried.

A segmented hat block impressed with "1897 CAPWO PAT BLOCK." This is believed to be the block for a woman's hat. *Courtesy of The Atwater Kent Museum.*

The Boss Raw Edge

For most soft hats, curling the brim was one of the final operations. However, with the Boss Raw Edge hats, the curling of the brim was done in the blocking department. Once the brim was flattened and trimmed to its exact width, hot water was applied to the brim. Manipulating the shrinking brim by hand, a curl was set in the brim that would withstand almost any weather conditions. Once the curl was set, as was the case with all hats, the Boss Raw Edge hat was first plunged into cold water and then dried.

Separating Soft and Stiff Hats

In the early stages, soft and stiff hat bodies passed through the same departments together; but, at this point the soft hats were sent to the pouncing room while the stiff hats went on to the press room.

Applying stiffening compounds to felt bodies to create stiff hats.

Finishing

Soft hats in the pouncing department were roughly finished mechanically, the crown and brim finished by separate machines. The inside of the crown was singed and another machine beat and brushed the dust out of the hat. The soft hat was now prepared for the finishing department.

In the finishing department, the soft hat was pulled onto a block, steamed, sponged, and ironed. Then it was carefully rubbed with emery paper to give the felt a smooth feel. The quality of the finish depended entirely on the skill of the finisher. The brim was ironed flat and cut to the proper width.

Pulling out felt hat crowns and brims.

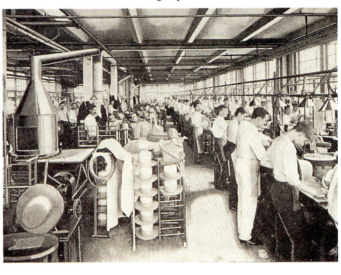
Applying the finishing touches to soft hats in the finishing department.

Curling the Soft Hat's Brim

With the exception of the Boss Raw Edge hats previously mentioned, curling the soft hat's brim is accomplished in the flanging department. The edge of the brim is moistened and turned up with a small, heated iron, and the hat is adjusted on a hollow wooden form, the brim fitted on a rim or flange of the required shape. A machine lowers a large, heated sand bag down onto the form, molding the brim into the exact shape of the flange within minutes.

Curling soft hat brims. Flanges are clearly visible at work on the left hand side of the photograph and idle beneath the large heated sand bags on the right. *Courtesy of the Pennsylvania State Archives.*

A curved iron for curling brims. *Courtesy of The Atwater Kent Museum.*

A crimping iron. *Courtesy of The Atwater Kent Museum.*

Trimming

Hats received their bands, binding, and leathers (sweatbands) in the trimming department at this point. Many different bow designs and binding styles were available. Once the bands, bindings, and leathers were properly fitted and inspected, the hat returned to the flanging department where it once again went under the hot sand bag prior to packing.

Women throughout the room are trimming soft hats.

Pressing and Finishing Stiff Hats

Pressing and finishing stiff hats was a labor intensive process requiring a great deal of handling. From the blocking department, stiff hats were sent to the press room where they were singed and brushed. The brims were cut to size and the hats were softened in an oven. Limp hat bodies were adjusted in iron molds, the brims were fitted with a bronze templet, and the hats moved on to hydraulic presses. A heavy rubber bag was forced into the crown and around the brim under two hundred and forty pounds of pressure, shaping both crown and brim. The turned edge of the brim was then planed automatically into the desired profile.

The men on the right are finishing stiff hats.

Stiff hats were finished in much the same way as soft hats, except that stiff hat finishers used lathes during the process. Finished hats were sent to stitchers, who machine-stitched one edge of the binding to the brim. These partially bound hats were sent to the stiff hat trimming department and the trimming was completed by hand.

As a final step, the curling department checked for any irregularity in the curl of the brim. Once the brims were adjusted to conform to the pattern, the stiff hats were packed for shipment.

Straw hats were also fashioned on blocks. Straw was usually braided and the braids were sewn together to create the hat. Straw hats were stiffened as well, using a sticky substance called sizing. Many consider the panamas to be the best straw hats, reputed to have been made from the jipijapa and toquilla fiber plants grown in Columbia. Here is one example of a straw hat block, appropriately labeled. *Courtesy of The Atwater Kent Museum.*

This Stetson Genuine Panama Select straw hat has a reddish band and dates from c. 1940. In the summer of 1941, the Stetson Company reported that they were making straw hats "with bands ranging from somber black to most violent Polynesian hues." Note the weave pattern on the crown of the Panama. *Courtesy of The Atwater Kent Museum.*

Auxiliary Departments

Every item needed to complete and ship a Stetson hat was produced within the walls of the factory complex. Silk for hat trimming was woven on Stetson looms. Tanned sheep, goat, and calf skins from Belgium, England, France, and Russia in a variety of colors entered the plant to be cut for sweatbands. Factory personnel also printed sweatbands with the manufacturer's trademark and often with dealers' names. Hot presses stamped the imprints onto the bands in gold or silver leaf. Blocks and flanges were also produced in the plant by pattern makers who carefully shaped them.

Now that we are familiar with basic hat terminology and the hat manufacturing process, we may move on to the history of John B. Stetson and his company. Following this Philadelphia company from its beginnings in 1865 to its close in 1970, the changing hat fashions of various decades will be discussed along with the firm's later diversification into other clothing lines.

Women and men working together to manufacture paper hat boxes at the Stetson plant.

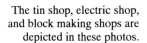

The tin shop, electric shop, and block making shops are depicted in these photos.

Chapter II

The History of John B. Stetson and His Company

The Early Years — 1830-1870

John Batterson Stetson was born in East Orange, New Jersey in 1830. His father, Stephen Stetson, was a successful hatter and taught his children the hatting trade. His family ran the No Name Hat Company in East Orange, established by Stephen in 1790 on Main Street. The company was known for its superior quality hats and "John B." learned the trade well as a child. As one of the most junior of thirteen siblings, however, John B. was unlikely to inherit the family business his brothers Henry T. and Napoleon and nephew Henry continued to run in 1850.[1]

"Westward Ho!"

John Stetson developed tuberculosis as a young man. He headed west to St. Joseph, Missouri, hoping to recover. His health was so precarious that he was rejected when he attempted to join the Union Army in the early 1860s as the Civil War was heating up.

St. Joseph was little more than a trading post outfitting parties bound for Pike's Peak and other points on the western frontier. Unable to leave town as a soldier, Stetson worked his way up to part owner of a brickyard on the banks of the Missouri River instead. When the river flooded and washed this business away, Stetson joined one of the groups headed west to Pike's Peak seeking their fortunes mining for gold. During the 750 mile trek on foot, John B. recovered his health.[2]

As the story goes, Stetson and his compatriots were sleeping rough, out under the stars. Occasionally they would sew together skins of animals they had killed, making crude shelters for rainy nights out on the open prairie. However, these untanned skins were worse than useless when the temperature rose the next morning. Seeking a less pungent form of waterproof shelter, Stetson used his felting skills to create waterproof tarps for himself and his partners.[3]

To make the felt, Stetson would have had to first shave the fur off a number of animal skins. Once he had a pile of fur, he would have made a hunter's bow from a hickory sapling and an animal skin thong. Following age-old techniques, he stirred the fur into a small, misty cloud. Drifting down in a fine, evenly distributed layer, Stetson gently blew a mouthful of water over the fur to bind the fibers together.[4]

When the fur mat was strong enough, Stetson rolled it up. Dipping the sheet of matted fur into a pot of boiling water, the mat shrank, pulling the fibers closer and more firmly together. When the process was finished, Stetson had a crude, water repellent felt blanket.[5]

Using this primitive felting technique, Stetson also fashion a large, broad-brimmed, open-crowned, "picturesque," modified sombrero for himself as additional shelter from the elements. As their travels continued, a cowboy is said to have spied Stetson and his unusual hat, rode up, tried the hat on for himself, and paid Stetson for it with a five dollar gold piece, riding off with the first Stetson western hat on his head. This was the original Boss of the Plains that would later become the cornerstone of Stetson's Philadelphia hatting business.

One year searching for gold in the shadow of Pike's Peak was enough for Stetson. In 1865, as the Civil War drew to a close, he returned East to Philadelphia to try his hand at the hat manufacturing trade he had been brought up on.

The young man in this tin type photograph is decked out in western garb, including a Boss of the Plains style hat. "Green Still" is written in pencil on the back of the tin type. Many old Stetson western hats found their way back East in the late nineteenth century. If a man went out West and didn't like it, he came back East. To save face, he brought a lot of gear back with him to make it look as if he had done well on his adventure. Stetson hats, expensive as they were, would have gone a long way to creating the image of success he hoped to project. *Courtesy of the Peter C. Schubert collection.*

Philadelphia Hat Manufacturing — 1865

The city John Stetson returned East to was a major metropolis in 1865. It had many large, mechanized factories, a sizable labor force regularly augmented with a steady influx of immigrants, inner-city slums, numerous commuters, and expensive residential and shopping districts.[6]

Philadelphia was known as a hat manufacturing town. Just prior to the Civil War, the city could boast of manufacturing some of the best hats in white fur felt and high quality silk.[7] According to 1860 Census figures, annual hat manufactures in the city of Philadelphia were valued at $1,109,000.[8]

Hats were being produced in Philadelphia for both domestic and foreign consumption. Many fashionable shops within the city's limits sold hats produced in city factories. Stetson would face serious competition from previously established hatters. However, the hat manufacturing process itself had yet to be consolidated under one roof in a single, efficient operation at the time of Stetson's arrival. Workers tended to drift from plant-to-plant and town-to-town.

Early Hat Making Attempts in Philadelphia — 1865-1866

In 1865, Stetson rented a small room at Seventh and Callowhill Streets. With investment capital of $60 loaned to him by his older sister, Louisa Stetson Larrick of Corwin, Ohio, he purchased his tools and fur, and took on two workers. Stetson's first hats were imitations of popular styles of the day. Their claim to fame was that they were lighter weight than most, a mere two ounces at a time when heavy felts called "iron" hats were the rule. Stetson wore his creations while traveling from one hat shop to another looking for sales. The results were less than stellar.[9]

The competition in the mid-range city hat market proved to be highly competitive. Stetson soon realized that if he were to stay in business he would have to try something different. Of course, he had already made something different ... out west.

The Stetson factory at 4th Street and Montgomery Avenue in Philadelphia as it appeared in 1870. *Courtesy of The Atwater Kent Museum.*

Success with the Boss of the Plains — 1866-1870

Texas cattlemen had become prosperous businessmen in the 1840s, driving as many as 200,000 longhorns over the Shawnee Trail to Missouri. Steamboats carried other herds across the Gulf of Mexico to New Orleans. When Civil War tore America, the drives stopped, cattlemen went off to fight the Yankees, and unattended herds doubled in size. After four years of war, ranchers returned to find huge, feisty, unbranded herds ranging across the plains. Here was a serious business opportunity.[10]

By 1867, the railroads reached as far west as Abilene, Kansas. Both railroad workers and Easterners were quickly supplied with cowboy-driven herds of Texas beef. In the early 1870s, railroads carried beef east and wealthy hunting parties west to slaughter buffalo herds, clearing the plains for additional steer. New rail lines continued westward and forts began to dot the landscape. Income levels out west were rising rapidly.[11]

With the Eastern hat market difficult at best, Stetson turned his attention to the Westerners. He acquired lists of clothing and hat dealers in the West. Extending his credit to the limits, Stetson made a western hat for each Southwestern dealer in the Boss of the Plains ("B.O.P.") style he had invented during the trek to

Pike's Peak. These hats were natural in color with four inch crowns and brims; a plain strap was used for the band. Stetson sent each dealers a hat and a letter asking for an order of a dozen. Within two weeks orders began to come in. Some of the orders came with cash, asking that their hats be delivered fastest. Stetson filled orders and sent out more sample hats with letters stating that prepaid orders would be filled first. While he was only making one style of hat, Stetson offered his "B.O.P." in different qualities ranging from one-grade material at five dollars apiece to extra fine nutria or pure beaver felt hats for thirty dollars each.[12]

As business picked up, the factory began to grow. *Courtesy of Irene Centofanti.*

Stetson had made the right choice. Elbert Hubbard tells us that in "... less than a year after Stetson began to make the B.O.P. hat he gave up Philadelphia local trade entirely, and in the interest of economy moved from the business district to 4th Street and Montgomery Avenue ... three miles out ... clear in the suburbs of the city." He purchased a three story building, one hundred feet long and thirty feet wide.[13] Stetson's grand nephew, John B. Stetson, described the early evolution of the 4th Street factory:

> ... my grandfather, George Arthur Stetson came from his father-in-law's farm (Lyons Farm outside of Elizabeth, New Jersey) to help his older brother John set up a factory to make hats. They bought a row house at 4th and Montgomery Avenues in Philadelphia from which they made and sold their hats. Soon they bought the house next door, and then the one next to it. But my grandfather had to leave John B. and go back to his wife and family because his father-in-law had died. He told John B. that his business was big enough — they had bought the last house in the row and knocked out the walls between all of them![14]

George Arthur Stetson was wrong. John B. would not stop building on that site until, by the early twentieth century, he would have the world's largest hat factory, with 25 buildings, connected by aerial walkways, covering 9 acres of ground.[15]

Stetson Company Boom Years — 1870-1920

The image of John Batterson Stetson that most people are familiar with. *Courtesy of the author's collection.*

Company Growth

In the early years, Stetson designed and manufactured his own hats. He also opened up sales territories for himself, promoting and marketing his own hats. The 1872 catalogs may have been his first. In the early 1870s seasonal catalogs, Stetson displayed his dress hats. These catalogs were sent to his retailers, with whom Stetson maintained close contact.[16]

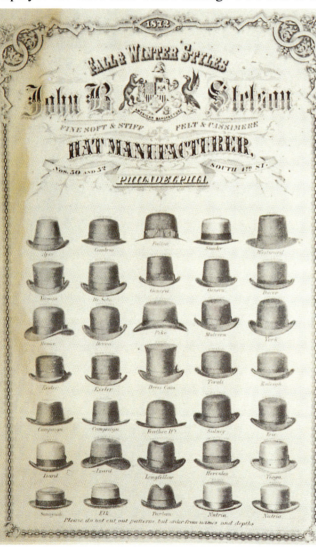

This was the 1872 Stetson catalog, displaying the company's dress hats. *Courtesy of Irene Centofanti.*

Every manufacturing step necessary to produce Stetson's hats was completed within the walls of the growing factory compound. By 1899, eight manufacturing departments would be involved in Stetson hat production. Even equipment was to be produced on site. The machine shop was one of the earliest departments completed, building and maintaining the factory's machinery.[17]

Aside from trapping and skinning animals, all stages of felt production and hat finishing occurred within the plant. Baled furs were processed into felt using company stripping and matting machines. While most firms believed nutria to be too expensive a fur for most hats, Stetson made a specialty out of manufacturing nutria soft felt hats.

Company weaving machines produced straw. Massive looms wove millions of yards of bands, bindings, and braids from raw silk, and a humidifying system added strength to the silk fibers, easing their passage through the looms.

Skins from calves, goats, and sheep were processed into sweatbands. These were imprinted with either gold or silver company trademarks with varying designs to indicate different qualities of hats. Box labels, order forms, stationery, and advertising materials were all printed in the company's commercial printing department.

Blocks and flanges were produced in house. Stetson's distinctive hat boxes were manufactured in the paper-box department, along with the cardboard rings and stays which supported the hats within the boxes.

Even building construction was an in house job. Company staff, and Stetson family members, erected the structures under the watchful eye of the company's architectural engineer.[18]

This self-contained company grew and prospered. The period between 1870 and 1920 was the Stetson Company's boom time, most of it under the direct supervision of John B. himself.

In 1880, some aspects of plant operations were still fairly primitive. No drying room had yet been built for the plant and hats were hung on iron pegs over the boilers to dry.[19]

Three years earlier, in 1877, Stetson's began to attract attention overseas. The first foreign orders came in from England and Japan. The English retailer's order was for $51.50 and the Japanese firm ordered $375.15 worth of hats. Whether these were dress or western hats was not recorded. Searching for Stetsons with foreign retailers' names printed in the sweatbands could become a fascinating preoccupation.[20]

Early International Business[21]

Year	Nations
1878	3 Canadian Retailers
1881	Germany
1890	Mexico, Canada, London & Hawaii
1891	Nicaragua
1893	Buenos Aires
1894	Havana, Cuba
1894-1895	Australia, New Zealand
1895	Italy

The complete Stetson factory as it appeared from 1915 until the early 1940s. This was a sprawling complex of 25 buildings that covered 9 acres of ground. *Courtesy of the Pennsylvania State Archives.*

In 1899 roughly 2800 retailers across America were selling Stetsons. While the hats were expensive to carry, merchants could rely on the fact that very few "dead stock" or shopworn hats would have to be sold at a reduced price. The hats arrived in good condition and apparently moved off the shelves quickly despite their high prices.[22]

To supply these retailers, the company employed over 1200 workers in 1899. Hat production was estimated at over 50,000 dozen hats for that year.[23]

Although John Stetson himself died in 1906, his company continued to prosper in the early twentieth century. By 1915 the 25 building factory covered 9 acres of ground, employed 5400 people — 4000 men and 1400 women, and was producing 3,336,000 hats annually, roughly 11,000 hats every day. These were supplied to 10,000 retail merchants and 150 wholesale distributors. Roughly 1125 of the retail merchants were in foreign countries that year, including Argentina, Europe, and South Africa.[24]

After the Stetson factory was established, the company opened a factory-owned retail store in Philadelphia to sell their hats. While other city merchants would carry Stetsons, only one such factory-owned Stetson Retail Store would ever operate in the city at one time. The first such shop was located in the 1100 block of Chestnut Street (a printed 1900 trademark with this store address has been recorded). On February 13, 1913, this shop was replace when the Stetson Company opened a new retail shop at 1224 Chestnut Street. For over half a century, the Stetson Retail Store at 1224 Chestnut Street would sell and renovate hats for mayors, governors, congressmen, senators, presidents, and any number of social luminaries who stopped by, as well as for everyday folk.[25]

A brown Royal DeLuxe Stetson labeled with the address of the Chestnut Street Retail Store, "John B. Stetson 1224 Chestnut Street Philadelphia." *Courtesy of Patty Stetson.* $75-100

The Stetson Company had retail shops in various cities around the United States and around the world. These shoes (manufactured by The Davenport Shoe Company of Butte, Montana) were sold in a Stetson retail shop, as shown by these "The Stetson Shop" cloth labels. *Courtesy of Elmer and Jan Diederich.*

Photographs of Stetson retail shops and offices as they appeared in 1925 in New York, London, Paris, and Chicago. The New York offices opened at 26th Street and 5th Avenue in 1922 and moved to 34th Street and 5th Avenue shortly thereafter. The Chicago office opened in 1924. *Courtesy of The Atwater Kent Museum.*

John B. Stetson's Paternalism Toward Employees

When John B. Stetson set up shop in Philadelphia, hatter's were not generally held in high regard. Nineteenth century hatmakers were known for their heavy drinking—said to wet the dry throats they developed working in dusty factories—and their job-switching ways. Hatmakers would be among the forefront of the union movement. Hatmakers were also considered snobbish, lazy, and careless with their money.

None of these attributes would produce the well-made, quality hats Stetson had in mind for his company. He needed workers who would stay on the job in his plant, who would remain sober, and who would be loyal to their employer. Stetson took some very unusual steps for a nineteenth century manufacturer to ensure that his hatmakers would be different. Both employer and employee benefited from the relationship.

Stetson developed an entire community in the lower Kensington district of Philadelphia where his factory was built. The company quickly became more than a source of employment for immigrant workers; for workers and their family members Stetson became a way of life, and the surrounding neighborhood row houses acted

as a company town. During this period of self-made industrialist millionaires, owners set the rules for life both in and outside of their plants.

Stetson followed suit. He took a paternalistic interest in the welfare of his employees, initiating a variety of company services from health care, education, and recreation, to banking, housing and religious services. Stetson was motivated by deep Baptist religious convictions, a strong philanthropic conscience, and a certainty that satisfied workers would be more productive. Employee benefits reduced labor turnover, attracted a higher caliber work force, and therefore increased the company's profits. As Roman Cybriwsky and Charles Hardy III wrote of Stetson's policies in 1981:

> From the 1870s to the 1920s the firm functioned under a labor-management system which in many ways was reminiscent of European feudalism.[26]

The company's paternalistic interests were not always all that benevolent, at least to modern eyes. Restrictions in their apprenticeship papers from the early twentieth century include, "[the apprentice] will not contract matrimony within the said term; that he will not play at cards, dice or any other unlawful games ... and that he will not absent himself day or night from his Masters' service without their leave, not haunt ale houses, taverns, or play houses ..." These terms are from the apprenticeship papers of Daniel Petrilli, dated December 28th 1919. He was to begin working in the Sizing Department for $7.00 per week. (During the early twentieth century, Italian immigrants most often found themselves beginning their employment in this department.) The papers were signed by J.H. Cummings, the company president. *Courtesy of Jean Vicoli.*

As the years passed, new services and programs continued to be added by Stetson. One of the most significant was the Union Mission Hospital, founded in 1887. Built next to the factory at 1745 North 4th Street, this facility was built in part because of Stetson's own preoccupation with health and from his habit of referring sick employees to his own personal physician. This fully equipped facility was capable of handling 20,000 patients each year and served the neighborhood as well as Stetson workers, who enjoyed reduced rates. This, of course, extended goodwill toward the firm out into the community and brought in new employees.[27]

Stetson organized nondenominational Sunday school and Tuesday morning prayer services at the plant, also available to the community at large. These services were strictly voluntary and Sunday school class enrollment swelled to between 500 and 700 congregants weekly, the largest assembly in Philadelphia.[28]

Especially important to employees was the Stetson Building and Loan Association. The Association provided loans and mortgages to workers, damping hatters traditional wanderlust and settling workers near the plant. Here they quickly became part of an expanding community with a growing number of Stetson activities with which to include their families. Stetson influenced the design of some of these houses, insisting on maximizing light and air flow. His efforts won Stetson national recognition.[29]

Stetson's grand nephew, John B. Stetson, illustrated how his grand uncle's programs worked ... and extended to his own relatives. Prior to relating this story, Mr. Stetson confided that while his grand uncle was very considerate of his workers, he grew more stern, or more determined, as he grew older.

> The oldest of George Arthur Stetson's [J. B. Stetson's brother] sons was my father Willis George Stetson who decided he did not want to work for his uncle John but went to work for Nathan Snellenburg, a large department store in Philadelphia. One day Nathan came to where my father was working with my father's hat in one hand and a pay envelope in the other. Said he, "Willis, your uncle has made it clear to me that you belong at the hat factory. I think you should do as he says." With that he politely ushered my father out to the street corner from which he caught a trolley to 5th and Montgomery Avenues, the main office of the hat company. Needless-to-say he was ushered in to John B.'s office where he was told he would begin as an apprentice at the magnificent sum of two dollars fifty cents per week.
>
> At that time everyone was paid at the end of every week, and come the following Friday my dad received his first pay envelope. In it he found two silver dollars, but no fifty cents. He was so mad he stormed right by John B.'s secretaries and into his uncle's office, claiming he had been robbed! John B. quieted him down and stated that each week fifty cents was going into a credit union account. This took a bit of selling since my dad was unmarried and having a good time at the Saturday night socials going on in the Stetson auditorium. By this time (1900) the hat factory was a community unto itself. It had its own commissary (soon discontinued during World War I), its own hospital, fire station, company hat store where employees got about 40% off list, and its own Sunday school in part of the auditorium. John B. had many distinguished speakers come to speak on Sunday, and had Sunday services along the lines of the Baptist Church since he was a Baptist from Russell Cornwell's Temple Baptist Church (from whence sprang Temple University).

The first Stetson Auditorium was in use until 1906.
Courtesy of The Atwater Kent Museum.

> My father met my mother at one of the Saturday night socials and they were married in 1905. The money saved in the credit union was a substantial down payment on their first home, built at John B.'s insistence in Melrose Park, about 10 blocks from his estate in Elkins Park.[30]

Company foremen and executives receive their Christmas bonuses for 1924 from President Cummings himself. *Courtesy of the author's collection.*

These men were preparing turkeys at the Stetson plant in 1924; the birds were Christmas gifts for the company's married men. *Courtesy of the author's collection.*

Referring to one of the many programs Stetson developed for the families of his workers, his grand nephew relates, "In about 1896-1897 John B. organized his own drum and bugle corps. They practiced on his estate in Elkins Park. He furnished everything — complete uniforms, shoes, instruments, etc. My father didn't play any instrument, so he carried the flag!"[31]

At the heart of Stetson's paternalistic policies was the company Christmas party. These were annual extravaganzas involving every employee and all of their family members. Congregating in the company auditorium, attendees witnessed speeches, prayer, musical performances, and were awarded gifts and bonuses. At the 1920 party, workers received ten percent of their annual salaries as bonuses. Turkeys were given to married men, hats to bachelors, and gloves and candies for the women employed by the firm. Also included among the gifts were 425 shares in the Stetson Building and Loan Association, 75 shares of common stock, and 5 life insurance policies worth $5,000 each. The total value in gifts given that year was $525,000. Gold watches were also commonly given as gifts, inscribed with the names of the recipients.[32]

Shares of common stock were also presented as Christmas gifts. Two shares of Stetson common stock, dated October 4, 1928. *Courtesy of the author's collection.* $18-22

Some of the company activities which took place in the Stetson auditorium in 1925 look a little odd today. *Courtesy of the author's collection.*

Stetson's philanthropy extended beyond the bounds of Philadelphia. At the urging of his second wife, Stetson purchased a large estate in DeLand, Florida in 1886—a community known as a haven for retired Baptist missionaries. There he endowed the struggling DeLand Academy with over $300,000. As a trustee he contributed freely to the institution, which in 1889 was reorganized as the John B. Stetson University, a Baptist institutions known for its solid law school today.[33]

Stetson's final project was the completion of a new 5,500 seat auditorium in 1906, the year of his death. Many company activities took place there, including political speeches, orations by visiting dignitaries who were having hats fitted, and concerts by the Philadelphia Orchestra.

All of these efforts strengthened the bonds between Stetson and his employees, creating a loyal, efficient work force, and ensuring stability among a traditionally wandering community.[34] Stetson's programs were continued by his successor, J. Howell Cummings (company president from 1906-1928). After World War I, Cummings expanded the programs, institutionalizing an extraordinary array of services which would be the forerunner of many company benefit packages.

These programs included a food cooperative servicing 1400 members by May 1920, group insurance for all employees with the company over 3 months, a Stetson Boy Scout Troop, a dental clinic, company chorus, a cabin for company outings, and a company paper called *The Hat Box*, for which the employees acted as reporters.

The first auditorium was replaced in 1906, the year of John B. Stetson's death. In this photograph, the company staff and their families take in the annual Christmas extravaganza, c. 1910. *Courtesy of Patty Stetson.*

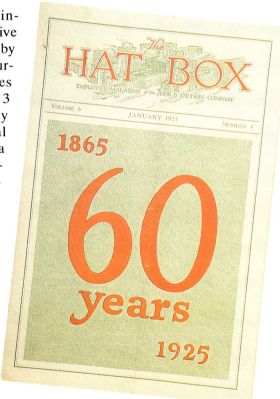

The January 1925 issue of *The Hat Box. Courtesy of the author's collection.*

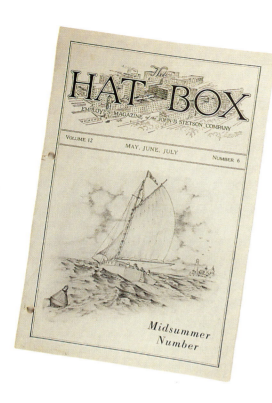 

The midsummer, 1931 edition of *The Hat Box*, extolling the virtues of a new reinforced edge for hat brims. *Courtesy of The Atwater Kent Museum.*

The Stetson Company management preferred to hire workers from the families of their current employees. This apprenticeship paper dated from 1915 illustrates the point. The father, Frank Petrilla, brings his son, Leonard, into the firm as an apprentice to Henry H. Roelofs of the Sizing Department. Leonard Petrilla's wages were listed as $2.00 per week. *Courtesy of Jean Vicoli.*

As Philadelphia was a city with a high immigrant population, the Stetson Company instituted Americanization classes. These seven-week courses in the English language, American government and history culminated in group trips to city hall where these students were sworn in as American citizens. In 1919, the Stetson Company had 247 unnaturalized immigrant employees. By 1921 all but three had become United States citizens, completing the Stetson classes.[35]

The company also encouraged employees to participate in athletics on the company fields. The employees were to organize the leagues and the company would provide all of the equipment. Sports included tennis on grass courts, quoit, open air dances, baseball, track, and indoor jogging for executives. The baseball team was a member of the Philadelphia industrial league and once played the Parksburg Brooklyn Royal Giants, a black team from the New York area, well before the major leagues admitted black players. The Stetson baseball team also played clubs from Philadelphia's suburbs and demonstration games against the Philadelphia Phillies.[36]

Extra attention was paid to the welfare of children growing up near the Stetson plant. They were seen as the future of the firm and needed to be socialized in the Stetson system as early as possible. Many educational and entertainment programs were offered in the company auditorium, along with sporting events of the ball field. Any celebrity who came to Stetson for a fitting was likely to put on a small performance or a mini-rodeo for the local children while he or she was there.[37]

Despite the fact that employees and would-be employees alike understood that these programs came out of their wages, as a direct result of these employee benefits begun by John Stetson and continued by Cummings, the company had a waiting list of job applicants. The Stetson Company preferred to hire relatives of employees and it was common for extended families to be employed by the company. By 1920, 208 employees had been with Stetson for over 25 years. These policies created a family atmosphere and generated company loyalty; under these policies the majority of Stetson employees also felt no need for unions until well into the 1930s, despite the fact that textile workers led the way in union formation in the early twentieth century. Stetson created the programs to guarantee that he achieved the quality he wanted in both his employees and his hats.[38]

The Stetson Company's paternalism rubbed off on some of their retailers as well. In 1910, the Montgomery Wards catalog included the following offer regarding Stetson hats:

> If you are undecided as to just what style or dimension will become you, just remit the price you wish to pay for a hat, give us the size of your hat, say whether you have a full, medium, or thin face, your weight and height, and which you prefer (Stiff, Fedora, Novelty, or Western shape) and color desired, and leave the selection to us. We will refer to our experienced hat man who will select a hat that is sure to become you.[39]

This Stetson Select Quality bowler with a silk lining is a fine example of the Stetson Company's paternalism extending on out to the customers themselves. It was found with the original hat box, cleaning pad, and warning label — admonishing the owner to return the hat to the company for cleaning. This hat was sold at the 1224 Chestnut Street shop in Philadelphia. *Courtesy of John J. Twers.* $100-125

Select Quality label in the silk lining of the bowler. *Courtesy of John J. Twers.*

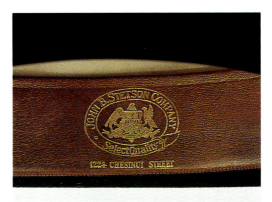

Select Quality label, gold impressed in the leather sweatband. *Courtesy of John J. Twers.*

Exhibitions

In 1876, the Philadelphia Centennial Exhibition linked the nation's celebration of its first century with a major exhibition of American industrial, innovative, and artistic strengths and invited all nations to participate. This was a bold move. Such exhibitions could easily become a source of fiscal and national embarrassment if crowds did not come or if the works of other nations outshone America's offerings.

However, if crowds did come, and for the Centennial Exhibition they most assuredly did, the opportunity for companies to display their wares to large groups of potential customers was irresistible in an age when mass advertising was difficult at best. As added benefits, manufacturers from all over the globe displayed a wide range of wares, offering the observant exhibitors an opportunity to tour international competitors exhibits and collect traditional manufacturing and stylistic techniques never before seen in the host country. New developments were widely and rapidly disseminated as never before. Also, products exhibited were judged and awards were presented. Prestige garnered by award winners translated into greater future sales. Some manufacturers created exclusive touring stock solely for these events.[40]

Stetson was not one to pass up such an opportunity. It is obvious that Stetson hats received both notice and awards at these international exhibits as Stetson participated in the Philadelphia Centennial Exhibition of 1876, the Paris Expositions of 1879, 1889, and 1900, the New Orleans Exposition of 1885, the Columbian Exposition at Chicago in 1894, the Omaha Exposition of 1898, and the National Association of Manufacturers' Exhibition in Caracas, Venezuela.[41]

Stetson's pleasure over winning international awards was evident in the open bragging his company indulged in after the 1889 Paris Exposition: "Stetson hats were so superior to anything shown, and aroused so much admiration among the French experts selected to judge hats, that they recommended the bestowal of one of these seven grand prizes to the manufacturers of Stetson hats. This action has a double significance when it is remembered that the prize was given to a foreign concern."[42]

In 1901, the Stetson company also printed trademark stamps in the hatbands for their stiff hats, premier and nutria quality stiff hats, and their flange brim and novelty hats which included the award medallions garnered by the company at the 1876 Centennial, and at the three Paris Expositions.

The Middle Years — 1920-1947

Growth and Depression

Throughout the 1920s, the Stetson company continued to do well. Immigration restriction acts of that decade may have cut into the company's labor pool. However, with the company's policy of hiring extended families, housing them around the plant, and raising their children in a Stetson culture probably limited the adverse impact of dwindling numbers of immigrants entering Philadelphia.[43]

In 1924, a listing of the departments makes it obvious that the Stetson Company kept every facet of hat production and factory maintenance in-house. The departments listed included:

Pouncing, Finishing, Soft Stock, Press Room, Flanging, Soft Packing, Trimming, Paper Box, Leather Printing, Commercial Printing, Office, Store Room, Cafeteria, Shipping, Machine Shop, Motive Power, Electricians, Tin Shop, Carpenter Shop, Painters, Fur Cutting, Forming, Sizing, Back Shop Expense, Blocking, Blockmaking, Sales, Soft Stiffening, Coloring, Second Sizing, Pulling Out, Apprentices (Finishing, Sizing, and Soft Stiffening), Bricklayers, Philadelphia Store, and New York Store.[44]

In 1925, Stetson and other hatters found themselves working against rising fur costs. During World War I, fur had been difficult to come by as most was procured from overseas sources and prices rose. After the war, the situation did not improve. A new competitor for furs had entered the market, dress

An old, nearly white TOM MIX Stetson. It features an old version the of The Last Drop From His Stetson advertising art and an imprint in the black leather band reading, "Sheplers Inc. World's Largest Western Store." It is also marked "TOM MIX." 6" high crown, 4" wide brim, and a 2" wide hat band. *Courtesy of the Cowboy Trader Gallery.* $300-500

makers. Dress makers were depleting stocks of rabbit and hare skins to manufacture fur garments. The amount of fur lost to them could never be accurately predicted by the hatters as a swing in fashion could demand dresses using larger or smaller amounts of fur in any given season. This began to make life difficult for Stetson, a company already manufacturing expensive fur hats and using 16,000,000 animal pelts in 1925 alone.[45]

During the 1920s, Stetson produced special hats for American Presidents and, the company claimed, for "the Presidents of most of the Republics of the world." Tom Mix, the popular movie star cowboy of the day, carried a trunk containing eighteen Stetsons with him during his travels to pass out to high government officials. In a 1925 Philadelphia visit, Mix presented one of his favorite Stetsons to Mayor Kendrick.

May 1926 window display. *Courtesy of The Atwater Kent Museum.*

Tom Mix was mimicking the work of Stetson salesmen all over the America in the 1920s. Traveling salesmen could be found in thirty cities at any given time during the decade, pushing the new season's lines. These salesmen came to town with a huge trunk full of hats, looking for the largest possible room in which to set up shop and display their wares. In large cities and towns, many hotels had rooms set aside for just this purpose, complete with street front windows, tables, and racks. In smaller towns and villages, salesmen had to make due with hotel basements, unrented store space, or even barns.[46]

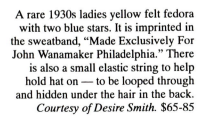

A rare 1930s ladies yellow felt fedora with two blue stars. It is imprinted in the sweatband, "Made Exclusively For John Wanamaker Philadelphia." There is also a small elastic string to help hold hat on — to be looped through and hidden under the hair in the back. *Courtesy of Desire Smith.* $65-85

Stetsons were still very popular in the 1920s. The Stetson Retail Store tore out their rear wall in 1924, extending their shop out to Samson Street to accommodated the growing numbers of customers visiting the shop.[47]

In 1930, Stetson opened a millinery department within the Philadelphia plant and began manufacturing women's dress hats. Two lines of hats were produced each year, featuring 200 styles. These hats were sold in the Philadelphia Stetson Retail Store, specialty shops, and department stores carrying Stetson hats.[48]

Stetsons would not continue to sell well in the 1930s. When the Great Depression hit the American economy, fewer and fewer people were interested in hats as fashion statements and cowboys made due with the hat they had. Many men decided to go altogether hatless during the Depression years.

In 1932 the Stetson Company responded with a lower priced unlined hat for $5.00, $7.50 lined, and reduced the prices on their established hat styles. As the prices dropped, Stetson asserted that its standards for high quality remained unchanged. The continuation of the hatless trend in post-Depression America, however, would eventually cripple the company that produced "the hat that won the West."

As domestic hat consumption declined, the American government's imposition of strong tariff barriers further hampered Stetson's. In 1935, as it became increasingly difficult to market their hats overseas, Stetson began setting up plants in other countries to thwart the tariff restrictions. Their first foreign plant was located in Canada. Stetson "acquired a substantial interest" in the Wolthausen Hat Corporation in Brockville, Ontario. One of the largest manufacturers of men's fur hats in Canada, Wolthausen producing Brock hats and other lines known throughout the Dominion. These continued to be produced, along with Stetsons. It was the first time Stetson hats had ever been produced outside of Philadelphia. Other foreign branches were soon opened in Mexico, Australia, and elsewhere.[49]

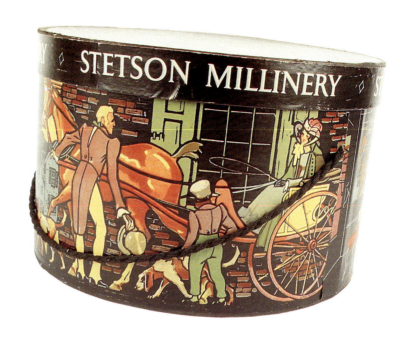

"Stetson Millinery" hat box with "American Made" printed on top. *Courtesy of The Atwater Kent Museum.*

Another problem facing the John B. Stetson Company in the 1930s was unfair competition from one Stephen L. Stetson, who began to peddle his own brand of hats, using the Stetson trade name, in 1931. These hats were manufactured by Hutt and Wasserman, Inc. in New York, given Stephen Stetsons last name only, and marketed misleadingly as Stetson hats. Stephen L. Stetson Ltd. was incorporated in 1933 and worked hard to convince retailers that there was a past connection between his company and the John B. Stetson Company and that his were legitimate Stetson hats. His Stetsons frequently contained "Certificate" labels to further mislead customers into thinking they were purchasing genuine Stetson hats.[50]

On March 26, 1936, a New York Circuit Court of Appeals decision against Stephen L. Stetson Ltd. and Hutt and Wasserman, Inc. brought this deceptive practice to a halt. These companies were found guilty of unfair competition and were forced to take their hats and advertising off of the market. A "Bob's Mens Store" of Chicago, Illinois was named as having sold the bogus hats.[51]

Keep an eye out for examples of these hats and their misleading advertising. The judge found an advertisement with the Stetson name and the word "Tradition" emblazoned upon it particularly deceptive. Both hats and advertisements alike were produced for five years before the courts forced this upstart New York firm to stop. While rare, there should be some examples of Stephen L. Stetson's handiwork and deceptive advertising on the market today.

Stetson's best years and Philadelphia's "golden age" as an industrial power both came to an end in the 1940s. In 1939, the company was using 15,000,000 animal skins, one million fewer than in 1925. In 1940, with the Philadelphia plant producing 400 different Stetson styles, the number of workers employed at the plant was down to 3,000—roughly 2,400 fewer employees than when the firm was at its height. Some, but not all, of this loss can be attributed to mechanization. However, even today hat manufacturers are using one hundred year old machines. There is simply not enough demand for hats to invest in or invent new hat manufacturing equipment, nor would there have been in the 1930s. As will be discussed later, some of this drop would be due to a loss of many of the programs which had ensured worker's loyalties when John Stetson ran the plant himself.[52]

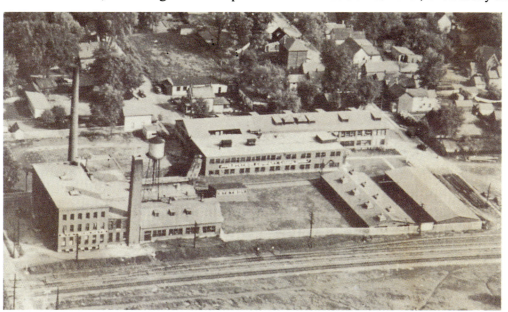

Stetson acquired a substantial interest in the Wolthausen Hat Corporation of Brockville, Ontario. *Courtesy of Irene Centofanti.*

The End of Paternalism and the Arrival of Unions at Stetson

In 1930, the John B. Stetson Company threw its last Christmas party. The 1930s saw an end to the close ties between management and labor that the company founder had been dedicated to, paternalistic practices were to be thrown aside for a new "scientific" approach to management. Adopting the recommendations of Philadelphian Frederick Winslow Taylor, working with the Wharton School of Business at the University of Pennsylvania and based on his studies at the city's Midvale Steel Company, Stetson Company officials eliminated "soft" jobs, replaced traditional hand processes with machinery, established a piecework pay system for all employees, and enforced more difficult work regimens for most company departments. These were unpopular moves, particularly for employees raised since childhood in the former Stetson culture and who had been working for the plant for many years.[53]

Further eroding relations between employees and management was the practice of laying workers off without pay during slow periods. In the hat trade there were two slow periods every year, in the winter and the late spring. Early in the Depression years, the company struggled to keep everyone employed, but business was dropping off with no signs of recovery; workers began to be sent home until needed without advanced notice of any sort.

The various employee benefit programs fell by the wayside as well, just as the Christmas bonuses had. By 1934 the workers brought demands for unionization, forming their first collective bargaining unit. The initial demand was a guaranteed minimum four hour work day. In 1936, the collective joined the United Hatters, Cap and Millinery Workers International Union.[54]

The tensions between labor and management continued to grow. This friction culminated in strikes in at the plant in 1936, 1937, and 1946.[55]

The John B. Stetson Company was now a union shop. Further distancing management and employees was the replacement of the Stetson Hospital with a Blue Cross-Blue Shield plan and the dismantling of the Stetson Mission Chapel in 1943. Following World War II, the rise of personal automobiles and rapid transit lines allowed workers to leave Stetson's former company town for the suburbs. Finally, over three decades, from the 1930s to the 1960s, Stetson management would farm out finishing and trimming operations to other companies across the United States. With that decision, all traces of John B. Stetson's original design for an efficiently run factory disappeared.[56]

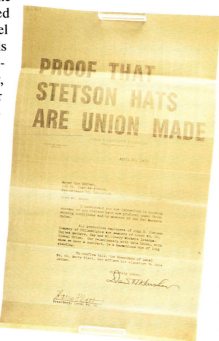

The John B. Stetson Company became a union shop in 1936. A "Proof That Stetson Hats Are Union Made" flyer dated April 23, 1959. *Courtesy of Irene Centofanti.*

War Conversion

World War II temporarily revived Philadelphia's flagging industrial economy. The shipyards, arsenal, and factories worked full bore, producing goods for the war effort. During the war years, Stetson sent their millinery department packing for New York and manufactured 20,000 Army campaign hats at $2.38 each. They also made hats for WAACs, webbing for the Army, Navy, and Air Corps, and parachute harnesses.[57]

Hatter's Highlights annual report, looking back over the year 1942. It includes hopeful photographs of soldiers returning home from World War II. The accompanying admonition reads "Keeping it under your Stetson will bring him home quicker." *Courtesy of Irene Centofanti.*

Hatter's Highlights contains a review of Stetson hats for 1942 and the company's contribution to the war effort. *Courtesy of Irene Centofanti.*

Employees serving in the military, from Hatter's Highlights. *Courtesy of Irene Centofanti.*

As part of the war effort, and in an attempt to convert the aging Stetson factory complex to a more modern single floor manufacturing design, the company tore down nine of their twenty-five buildings in May of 1943, reducing their factory space by 350,000 square feet. The buildings demolished had been built between 1891 and 1923, including the Chapel. From these structures, one of which was the eight story tall backshop where all of Stetson's hats had previously been formed, 4000 tons of scrap metal was recovered for military use, "enough metal for a heavy cruiser or 300 medium tanks," declared the Philadelphia papers.[58]

The Short Post-War Boom of 1947

Following the war, Stetson enjoyed a brief 50% rise in hat sales over 1941. On August 16, 1946, Stetson acquired the Mallory Hat Company of Danbury, Connecticut. The companies were operated separately, Mallory manufacturing all types of men's fur hats and women's fur felts. This added to sale and Stetson enjoyed a brief sales boom in 1947, achieving a postwar high of $29,300,000.[59]

Trouble was looming on the horizon. Fur prices had doubled between 1941 and 1946. Customers, however, were determined not to pay higher prices for their hats. In fact, many of the men who returned from war were sick of hats. They had been forced to wear them every day throughout the war and, now that they were out of the service, many were determined never to wear a hat again. While men and women laboring under western skies continued to need and buy western hats for protection, city folk no longer desired the don hats or caps as fashion statements or symbols of conspicuous consumption.

Many textile factories moved South to find cheaper labor after World War II. Service industries gradually replaced Philadelphia's heavy industry. The Stetson Company remained in their Philadelphia plant, but with the odds increasingly stacked against future success, they were on a long downhill slide toward licensing their name to others and closing their factory doors forever.[60]

Harry Pratt, once the president of the union at Stetson, is shown with two Mallory Hats displays from the 1960s. *Courtesy of Irene Centofanti.*

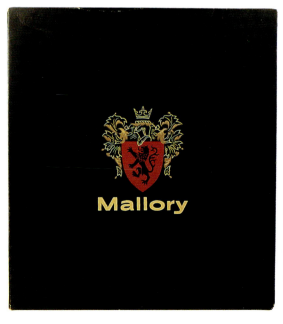

On August 16, 1946, Stetson acquired the Mallory Hat Company of Danbury, Connecticut. This is one example of the Mallory hat boxes. *Courtesy of Irene Centofanti.*

The Long Slide to Licensing — 1948-1970

Consolidation and Diversification

Despite the decline in the men's hat market, the John B. Stetson Company remained in the Kensington district of Philadelphia throughout the 1960s. Internal changes, consolidation of the companies resources, and diversification into other clothing lines kept Stetson afloat throughout this period.

After World War II, with sales declining, Stetson restructured the factory itself. Modern production methods demanded a one story, straight-through production line for maximum economy. Attempting to emulate this new standard, Stetson consolidated its operations into fewer buildings. Rising costs for raw materials, energy, a unionized labor force, and transportation were making it ever more difficult for the company to make a profit.

In 1950, Stetson sold its three story Philadelphia Retail Store property to the Prudential Insurance Company for $345,000 and took out a long term lease on the 19 x 235 foot lot to increase their savings while keeping the shop open. In May of 1951, Stetson returned the millinery division, moved to New York in 1941, to the Philadelphia factory as part of their consolidation plan. That year they were to produce two lines with 200 hat styles, mostly in felt, ranging from $10.95 to $24.95 in price. Within a few years, Stetson would close the millinery division altogether.[61]

By 1958, hatters were increasingly frustrated by the ever increasing numbers of hatless Americans. Stetson sales had dropped 32% since the brief boom of 1947. David H. Harshaw, the company president since 1947, put up a sign in the lobby of the head office which expressed his frustration: "To hatless salesmen, it will be to your interest to wear a HAT when visiting our plant. We are proud of our product, too." Even the salesmen could not be relied upon to wear a Stetson![62]

Many cite 1960 as the year when the last nail was driven into the coffin of the waning men's hat industry. On a frigid day in January 1960, the newly elected President John F. Kennedy took the oath of office and spoke to the nation hatless.

By 1964, Stetson had consolidated or eliminated much of its operation. Finishing and trimming operations farmed out to companies across America were returned to the Philadelphia plant, bringing about the closing of the Lee factory in Danbury, Connecticut, and the Alexander factory in Reading, Pennsylvania. Seven hundred jobs were eliminated in this move.[63]

Stetson initiated a diversification program in 1955 to increase sales. That year the J.B. Stetson Company paid $87,500 for a Stetson trademark owned by another manufacturer, producers of shirts ties, and pajamas. Another early step in their diversification program was to acquire the Stetson Shoe Company Incorporated of South Weymouth, Massachusetts, in 1964—a company founded in 1885 by one Ezra H. Stetson and A.C. Heald. Stetson would continue branching out into the clothing world until their name could be found on shoes, shirts, ties, pajamas, and underwear by 1970. Keep your eyes open for clothing carrying the Stetson label. Refer to the table for additional companies Stetson acquired and tagged with their label.[64]

Stetson-Acquired Clothing Concerns 1956-1970[65]

Company	Location	Product	Year of Acquisition
Young's Merchandising Corp.	New York City	Retail Men's Hat Stores	1955
James Fallar, Inc.	St. Albans, Long Island	Neckwear	1956
Fuller Shirt Co.	Kingston, NY	Shirts	1956/1957
Frank H. Lee Co.	Danbury, CT	Hats (Lee & Disney Brands)	1960
Better Made Headwear Co., Inc.	NY	Casual Hats	1968

In 1965 Stetson also entered into an agreement with the Elite Hat Manufacturing Company of Philadelphia to produce millinery for Stetson on a royalty basis. Stetson had abandoned women's hats in the early 1950s.[66]

Closing Down and Licensing the Stetson Name

By the late 1960s, the Stetson Company's days in Philadelphia were numbered. Hats sales declined steadily and additional clothing lines were not able to take up the slack. In mid-April of 1968, Stetson closed the Stetson Retail Store in Philadelphia. In the last years the store was open, millinery, men's furnishings, shoes, and sports coats bearing the Stetson trade name had been sold there. The next year, 1969, Stetson dropped a twenty year practice of giving mayoral candidates running in New York City a free hat to "toss into the ring." Stetson Vice President Louis Stetson Allen declared, "We are beginning to feel as though candidates are announcing just to get a free topper."[67]

By August of 1970, much of the company's property had been sold or leased, including the Fifth Avenue Stetson Store in New York City. The company that had once employed 5400 people was down to 800, had not made a profit in five years, had sold controlling shares in the company to a New York based firm named Ramco Enterprises, Inc., and was leasing 300,000 square feet of its 1,000,000 square foot factory complex to others. In October of 1970, Stetson management announced they would close the Philadelphia factory forever. By December 1970, only 300 employees remained.[68]

Over the decades, the Stetson Company had licensed fourteen overseas hatters to manufacture and sell hats bearing the Stetson trade name. By January 1971, the John B. Stetson Company was out of the hat business, its only remaining sources of revenue to come from royalties paid by the licensees using the Stetson trade name worldwide, rentals, and interest. The decision was made to license the Stetson name in America to a subsidiary of the Stevens Hat Manufacturing Company of St. Joseph, Missouri. The subsidiary became known as the Stetson Hat Group and Stetson's remaining inventory and equipment were sold to Stevens in return for payments over a number of years.[69]

The John B. Stetson factory complex at 4th and Montgomery Avenue was not successfully rented after the Stetson Company shut its doors and moved their licensing operation to New York. Industry had left Philadelphia and was not going to return. In May 1977, Stetson donated the real estate to the city of Philadelphia. In 1979 Philadelphia tore down the plant with the exception of three structures including the clock tower with a bell cast by the Whitechapel Foundry, the English firm responsible for the Liberty Bell, and the eight story front office and show room with golden John B. Stetson Company lettering decorating the facade. Plans were made to restore these structures as a reminder of Philadelphia's former industrial prowess. However, in 1980, arsonists destroyed this last remnant of the massive complex which had once produced the most famous icon of America's wild west, the cowboy hat.[70]

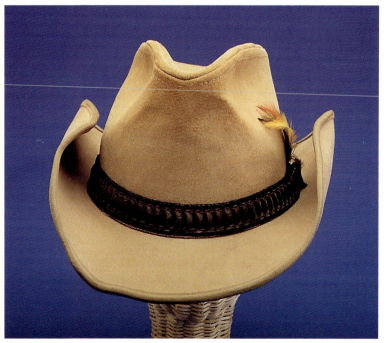

One of the western hats produced by the Stetson Group. The lining features the image "The Last Drop From His Stetson" in full color. *Courtesy of Joy Shih Ng.* $75-100

Stetson Lives On

John B. Stetson Company as Licenser

By 1986, the John B. Stetson Company of New York had attempted to diversify yet again, licensing the Stetson name to a wide variety of products including Cody and Lady Stetson colognes, millinery, luggage, handbags, umbrellas, and scarves. Reorganizing under Chapter 11 bankruptcy, the company replaced the president pushing diversification with Frances Guilden Gardner, daughter of Stetson's former Chairman Ira Guilden. She reduced the number of licensees and restricted the number of hat styles produced. Gardner stated, "We weren't really concentrating on the thing our name is so famous for ... Now we are concentrating on the hat business, which we had strayed away from ... [Stetson] is something I grew up with, and a great part of American heritage and a legacy, and I feel very strongly it's something we shouldn't let die."[71]

The Stetson Licensee

Stetson hats continue to be manufactured and sold in America. Ironically, they are now manufactured in the town, St. Joseph, Missouri, where John B. Stetson tried to set up a business and failed. In 1971, a small family business, the Stevens Hat Company, bought the license for the Stetson name, purchased the Stetson stock, equipment, and labels and continued to produce the western hats that originally made the Stetson name famous 105 years earlier.[72]

By 1979, the St. Joseph factory's 300 workers were manufacturing over 100 Stetson hat styles, ranging from $15 cloth hats to $200 high-grade beaver fur western hats. Unlike the original Stetson factory, the St. Joseph plant does not manufacture their hats all under one roof. The furs for felt hats are prepared in plants in Newark, New Jersey and Danbury, Connecticut.

Stevens received a boost in the mid-1970s when demand for hats rose. By 1981, 60% of the company's sales were western hats. The company was producing a smaller cowboy hat called the "East-West" for self-conscious suburban cowboys. It was described as having a sophisticated flair.[73]

The Stetson Hat Company Group and Hat Brands, Inc.

By the mid-1980s, the St. Joseph factory headquarters was now in Texas and the company name had changed to The Stetson Hat Company Group and their biggest seller was the "Indiana Jones Hat." The movie *Urban Cowboy* also pushed hat sales. At that time, Resistol Hats of Garland, Texas was the company's largest competitor, with the American Hat Company, Inc. of Houston and the Bailey Hat Company of Los Angeles close behind. In 1991, the "East-West" Stetson was still being manufactured. The purpose of the hat, as described by a Stetson salesman, was: "This is for the guy in Cherry Hill who's afraid to come out and empty his garbage in a western hat."[74]

As of this writing, the corporate name has changed again. Stetson hats are now manufactured in the St. Joseph, Missouri, plant by Hat Brands, Inc. Hat Brands also currently manufactures Resistol and Charlie 1 Horse hats, making it one of the largest manufacturers of headwear in the world.[75]

If you wish to purchase a modern Stetson, however, do not call Hat Brands. They only sell Stetson hats to retail merchants. You need to find the closest retailer carrying "the hat that won the West" if you want a new one. And be prepared to pay the price, Stetsons are still high-quality, high-priced hats.

For collectors and dealers, keep your eyes peeled. Fine old Stetsons turn up in the strangest places.

Chapter III

Men's Hats

"Nearly every civilized man wears a hat, and to most men the word 'hat' means 'Stetson'."
— Early twentieth century promotional claim

Hats of East and West — 1870-1920

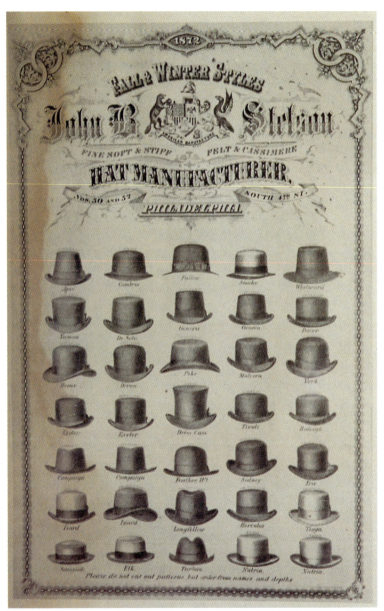

The company's 1872 catalog featured the men's dress hats available to retail merchants of the day. *Courtesy of Irene Centofanti.*

As America's economy boomed following the Civil War, many hard working families dreamed of becoming wealthy. Those who made their fortunes in industry, cattle, oil, and other ventures felt compelled to display their wealth on their bodies with fashionable clothes and hats. Middle class men aspiring to fortune and fame dressed for success as best they could.

Fashionable men with money to spend invested small fortunes on self adornment. Prosperous gents went to the best tailors and hatters to be properly dressed. A sharp hat was a man's pride-and-joy.

Stetson had decided to return to the hatter's trade he had been raised with at an opportune time. While his "staple hats" (western hats) were the foundation of his business empire, Stetson soon added dress hats to his product line. The demand for Stetson dress hats among the rich and rising middle class seeking to complete their fashionable attire soon outstripped the company's western production.

A western Stetson with the flat-brimmed, straight-sided crown with rounded corners "Boss of the Plains" style popular throughout the latter half of the nineteenth century and well into the twentieth. This example has an imprinted Stetson mark in the sweatband, without gold or silver in the mark. *Courtesy of the Peter C. Schubert collection.* $100-125

1870-1900

In the 1870s, there were many more hat styles available to men than would later be the case. This wide variety in hat style was meant to complement the vast array fashionable clothing men of this period wore to display their wealth. One fashionable hat of choice in the early 1870s was a smaller version of the top hat called a "chimney pot." Between 1870 and 1900, toppers, "wide awakes" (also referred to as Jim Crows in the United States), and bowlers were losing favor among men, being replaced by the homburg, a stiff felt hat with a deep crease running along the crown from front to back. The homburg was a personal favorite of Edward VII, the Prince of Wales. Another hat on the rise during this period was the trilby, a soft felt hat with a low, creased crown. The trilby was named for the hat worn by an actor named Beerbohm Tree who performed in a play by George du Maurier which also bore that name. Another popular, low crowned, center creased hat which took its name from a play was the fedora. The play *Fedora*, by Sardou, was first performed in 1881. Straw hats of this period were extremely popular summer wear, including the boaters.[1]

Western hats offered by Stetson from 1870 to 1900 included the Boss of the Plains, Alaska, Columbia, Dakota, and Railroad styles. In 1899, the Stetson Monthly declared that the Alaska and the Boss of the Plains were their two most popular "cowboy" hat styles. In 1900-1901, the Montgomery Ward & Company Fall and Winter catalog offered the Columbia, Dakota, and Railroad styles. The Columbia style was a medium sized and shaped hat, suitable for an "average size man." It had a 5 3/4" medium round crown, an 8" raw edged, flange brim, a 1/8" silk band, and a "Russia" leather sweatband. It came in either black or belly nutria colors and weighed 4 ounce. The Columbia sold for $3.75 each or $40.50 per dozen. A similar Columbia style hat, not manufactured by Stetson, was offered in the same colors and weight for $1.35, $1.75, and $2.25 each, or $14.58, $18.90, & $24.30 per dozen.[2]

The Alaska

The "Dakota" style was a full shaped, round-crown, broad-brim hat measuring 6" high at the crown and 8 1/2" wide at the raw edge brim. This hat was trimmed with a 3/8" silk band and Russia leather sweatband. This staple hat was considered a good choice "if you are a large man ..." It could be worn either creased or with a flattened, domed crown. The Dakota style was offered in black or belly nutria colors and weighed 5 ounces. It was sold for $4.00 each or $48.20 per dozen. Wards offered a similar Dakota style hat, not manufactured by Stetson, in the same colors with a 4 1/2 ounce weight for prices ranging from $1.40, $1.90, and $2.40 each to $15.12, $20.52, and $25.92 per dozen.[3]

The "Railroad" style hat was made with a nearly square top and a flat set brim. It measured 4 1/2" high at its full, slightly rounded crown and 2 3/4" wide at the flat set, bound edge, brim. A 1 1/8" wide silk band trimmed the hat. The Railroad had a Russia leather sweatband, weighed in at 4 ounces, and came in black or belly nutria colors. This hat sold for $3.50 each or $37.80 per dozen. Wards offered a similar Railroad style hat, not produced by Stetson, for $1.40 or $1.90 each and $15.12 or $20.62 per dozen.[4]

The Boss of the Plains

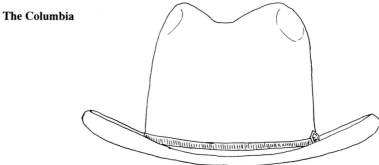

The Columbia

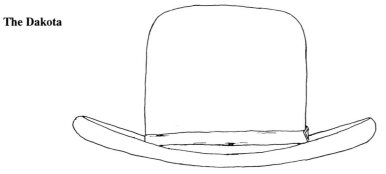

The Dakota

The Alaska, Boss of the Plains, Columbia, and Dakota staple (western) styles as they appeared in 1899. The Alaska of that year had a 4 1/2" high crown and a 3 3/4" wide brim. The Boss of the Plains measured 4 1/2" high and had a 4" wide brim; the Columbia had a 5 5/8" high crown and a 3" wide brim; and the Dakota measured 5 1/2" high at the crown and 3 1/2" wide at the brim. Be aware that the 1902 Sears catalog has misidentified the Columbia and Dakota, reversing the line drawings and descriptions.

1900-1920

Following men's fashions into the twentieth century were the top hat, bowler, homburg, fedora, and trilby. With the exception of the panama, no new men's fashion appears prior to World War I.[5]

In searching the Montgomery Wards catalogs by decades, Stetson hats were offered in 1890, 1900, and 1910. The 1910 listing was the largest and apparently the last decade Wards would offer Stetson hats. No mention was made of Stetsons in the 1920 Wards catalog. Stetson dress hats, derbies, novelty hats, bowlers were listed, all priced at $3.50 each. Seven Stetson western hats were also listed, varying in price from $3.50 to $7.00 each.[6]

The crown of the summer bowler is ventilated with holes in a Maltese cross pattern, puncturing the top of the crown. It was stamped with a merchant's name and address, "Harry Harold Hatter 6 & 8 So. Broad Street Trenton NJ." *Courtesy of John J. Twers.* $75-125

These are two fine examples of Stetson bowlers. While they may not date precisely within this time frame, they illustrate the type well. Stetson Comfort bowler, a summer bowler made without an interior lining to help keep the head cool. It was manufactured for Springarm Inc. of Jersey City. Stetson Comfort, printed in gold on leather band. *Courtesy of John J. Twers.* $75-125

One early Stetson hat designer observed that many held the view that men's hats just did not change over the years. He challenged that assumption, stating that they varied by as much as 1/8" in either the crown or the brim every year! The second example is a Stetson Special bowler with a 2" brim. It carried the retailer's imprint in the sweatband: Jack Reeds' Sons, Philadelphia. *Courtesy of John J. Twers.* $75-125 each

Black felt fedora marked "Royal DeLuxe Stetson, St. Regis, John B. Stetson Company & Carlton, Trenton." *Courtesy of Patty Stetson.* $75-125

Three derbies were offered. The first was listed as "very nobby medium shaped." It had a 5" high round crown and a 1 7/8" flat set brim with a slight curl. It was trimmed with a silk ribbon band and was considered a moderate shape intended for young or middle-age men. It was offered in black, pecan, or medium brown.[7]

The second derby was a larger shape derby hat "suitable for full faced or elderly men" It had a 5 1/2" high full round crown, a 2 1/2" wide brim with a heavy curl, and a grosgrain silk ribbon band. It was offered in black or seal brown.[8]

The third derby was the "Flexible Conforming Derby Hat for fall and winter." Being self conforming, it would "fit any head with comfort" and was said to "hold its shape longer than all others." The medium round crown measured 5 1/4" high and the curled brim was 1 3/4" wide. It was trimmed with a silk band, had a hand sewed leather sweatband, and was light weight and durable. It was offered in black only.[9]

Three Stetson novelty hats, the "Artist," "Placer," and a nameless "up-to-date novelty hat" were listed. The Artist was a flat crown telescope hat. It was listed as being very nobby (not a smooth felt), made of No. 1 quality fur. The telescoped crown was 4 3/4" deep; a 2 1/4" bound edge, brim with slight curl and genuine English leather sweatband finished the look. Stetson advised that this hat "looks best with the brim turned down in front." The Artist was offered in black and lead.[10]

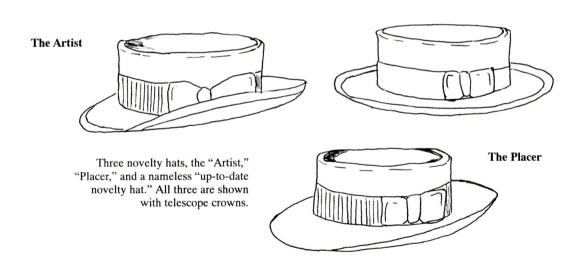

The Artist

The Placer

Three novelty hats, the "Artist," "Placer," and a nameless "up-to-date novelty hat." All three are shown with telescope crowns.

An example of the telescope style crown in a western hat with a bound brim. *Courtesy of Elmer and Jan Diederich.* $100-150

The Placer was "Stetson's Latest Novelty Style." It could be worn with either a dented or a telescoped crown. It was light weight and soft with a roll brim 2 1/2" wide, a raw edge, and had a 5" oval crown; the Placer also had a 2" silk band. Stetson further advised: "You will find it will produce the best effect turned down in front and crown dented." The Placer came in black and natural pearl colors.[11]

Stetson's "Up-To-Date Novelty Shape" was a rather large telescope hat: "the newest creation in hats for the coming season." It had a 4 1/2" crown, a 2 3/4" flat net brim, and a bound edge with a very slight curl. It was trimmed with a 1 3/4" good silk band. This hat came in Pearl Gray only.[12]

Two fedoras were offered. The first was a medium shape fedora hat using "Star Quality" fur (a term Stetson attached to flange brim and novelty hats of average price). This hat was suitable for those whose faces are not so full. It had a 5 1/4" round crown, a 2 1/4" bound edge curled brim, and a grosgrain silk sweatband. It was further described as "not an extreme hat but neat and attractive." This fedora was offered in black and Forest Green.

The second fedora had an almost square crown measuring 5 1/2" deep, a 2 1/2" curled brim, a bound edge, a silk ribbon band, and an improved leather sweatband. It was considered to be becoming to anyone. This fedora was sold in black & Tobacco Brown.[13]

The 1910 Montgomery Ward Catalog also included seven Stetson western hats. These were listed from the least to the most expensive. The first was the "Lenox," with a 5" medium round crown, a 8" rather flat set brim, a curled raw edge, a silk band, and a good leather sweatband. The crown could be worn dented or plain. The Lenox was offered black or side nutria colors at $3.50 each.[14]

The "Austral" was a nobby western hat with a flat set, raw edge brim measuring 3" wide and a 4 1/2" square crown. This hat was generally worn with the crown dented, sporting a good silk band and a leather sweatband. It was considered a popular dress hat among "railroad men, ranchmen, etc." It was guaranteed to be able to stand hard usage. It was offered in black and belly nutria for $3.75 each.[15]

The "Columbia" was "suitable for medium or large size men and is often worn as the regular marshal or police hat." It had a 5 3/8" rather high crown, a 3" curled brim, a raw edge, a narrow silk band, and a good leather sweatband. It came in two colors — black and belly nutria and was listed at $3.75 apiece.[16]

The "Dakota" was a "popular and staple shape for large men or those requiring a large hat, popular in the west and south..." It had a 5 3/4" full square crown, a 3 1/2" flat set brim with a curled edge, a narrow silk band, and a genuine leather sweatband. The Dakota was offered in black and belly nutria for $4.00 each.[17]

The "Round Up" was considered to be a "popular stockman's hat." It had a somewhat low 4 1/2" crown and a 3 3/4" stiff, flat double brim. A silk ribbon band and Russian leather sweatband finished the hat. It was generally worn with a dented crown and was offered in belly nutria color only. It was listed at $4.00 each.[18]

The "Provident" was described as an extra high grade Stetson hat, "strictly a Western or Southern hat." It had a 5 3/4" full crown, a flat set raw edge brim with a slight curl on edge, and a narrow silk band. This hat was recommended "for those requiring a large shape." It was offered in black & belly nutria for $6.00 each.[18a]

Finally, the most expensive Stetson western in the catalog was the "Rainer," an extra high grade genuine XXX Beaver hat "guaranteed for service." It had a 4 1/2" soft crown, a 3" flat, flexible brim, a silk bound edge, and a genuine Russian leather sweatband. It was offered in a belly nutria color only for $7.00 each.[19]

Hats From 1920 Onward

1920-1930

Following World War I, the top hat was reserved only for very formal occasions, replaced by the bowler as daily "power dress." The straw boater is largely replaced by the panama. The trilby or snap brim hat became the all purpose hat cutting across class strata in America and Europe. Narrowing the trilby's brim made it a less formal hat than its nineteenth century predecessor.[20]

Illustrations from the November 1925 issue of *The Hat Box*. The notables proudly portrayed in their western Stetsons include (left to right, by page) Tom Mix, Doug Fairbanks, Jr., Buck Jones, Hoot Gibson, Jack Hoxie, Red La Rocque, Lefty Flynn, and Hank Mann. *Courtesy of the author's collection.*

Cowboy actor Buck Jones owned this Stetson and had his name stamped in the band. He is shown wearing the hat in the 1925 illustration from *The Hat Box*. He is seen on the lower left of that illustration in the circular photo. *Courtesy of Mark Arrowsmith, Arrowsmith's Relics of the Old West ... $1500-2000 for a hat personally owned by Buck Jones.*

A 1925 Stetson Hats advertisement, featuring "The London" men's fedora. *Courtesy of the author's collection.*

A Stetson dress hat advertisement appearing on the April 1925 edition of *The Hat Box*. *Courtesy of the author's collection.*

Stetson caps available in 1926. *Courtesy of The Atwater Kent Museum.*

While none of the men's hats illustrated in the Sears catalogs presented here from the 1920s onward are Stetsons, the hat styles are similar to those produced by the Stetson Company. The catalog pages are presented here to help identify the changing hat styles across the decades. These pages are from the 1926 Spring and Summer Chicago catalog, pp. 220-221. © 1926, Sears, Roebuck and Co.

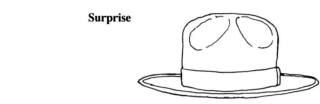

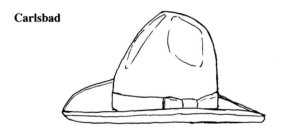

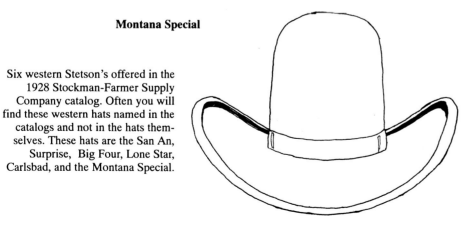

Six western Stetson's offered in the 1928 Stockman-Farmer Supply Company catalog. Often you will find these western hats named in the catalogs and not in the hats themselves. These hats are the San An, Surprise, Big Four, Lone Star, Carlsbad, and the Montana Special.

In the spring of 1928, the Stockman-Farmer Supply Company catalog from Denver, Colorado, offered six Stetson western hats. Each could be lined in satin for the additional charge of one dollar. The least expensive of the six was the "Surprise," a low 4 1/2" high crown, straight 3" wide brim, Number 1 quality felt hat in Belgian Beaver (light sand) color for $9.00.[21]

The "San An" was a Number 1 quality felt, "classy outdoor man's medium shaped hat" finished with matched band and binding. The crown measured 6 1/4" high and the brim was 3 1/2" wide, slightly tipped at the sides. The San An was also offered in Belgian Beaver (light sand) for $10.00.[22]

The "Big Four" was made in a smooth finish with a 6 1/4" full crown and a 4" brim. It was described as "a standard shape among western men for years." The Big Four was offered in Belgian Beaver (light sand), Number 1 quality fur for $11.00.[23]

The "Carlsbad" was one of the most popular hats for Stockman-Farmer. It had a 7" crown and 4" rolled brim with a raw edge. It was offered in Stetson's Number 1 quality felt, Belgian Beaver (light sand) and Tobacco brown colors for $12.00.[24]

The "Lone Star" was a Real Nutria quality felt hat offered in a very light creamy Buckskin (almost white) with a wide Tobacco Brown band and binding. "A real hat for men who are particular," measuring 7 1/2" high at the crown and 4 3/4" wide at the brim. The Lone Star cost $20.00.[25]

Stockman-Farmer's most expensive Stetson offering was the "Montana Special." It was one of the extra large hats made with a 7 1/2" high crown and a 6" wide brim. It was sold in Belgian Beaver (light sand) color and was made to order only. It was described as being of Stetson's Boss Raw Edge quality and sold for $30.00.[26]

A story in *The Hat Box* from May 1925 provides a useful tip for dating hats of this period sold at the Stetson Retail Store in Philadelphia, and possibly at other Stetson-owned stores. The upshot of the story was that a woman who had been robbed the year before had accused a prominent man of the crime who happened to live near by. She claimed she recognized him by his Stetson and convinced the judge with her certainty. The wife of the accused, however, remembered that her husband's hat had been purchased two weeks after the robbery. She and her lawyer returned to the Retail Store looking for the sales receipt as proof that the hat was purchased after the crime. The manager was able to produce the slip and an additional proof. The Stetson Retail Store was stamping the date of purchase in the sweatbands of every Stetsons sold in their shop. This was further proof that the accused could not be the man based on the evidence of his hat. It also suggests collectors and dealers should be peering more closely into Stetsons to see if there are purchase dates to be found on those sweatbands.[27]

1930-1939

The trilby was worn by nearly every man out-on-the-town or on business by the mid-1930s. Traditional cloth caps and tweed sports caps were common in the country.[28]

Men's hats offered in the Sears, Roebuck and Company Boston catalog for the fall and winter of 1938-39, pp. 454-455. © 1938-39, Sears, Roebuck and Co.

1940-1947

Mens' hats did not change much during the war years. Snap brims remain in style. Stetson reported in December of 1940 that high-crowned, brown, and gray derbies had almost disappeared completely and that "hard" (stiff) hats were on the way out. Stetson indicated that the biggest change in mens' hats in years was in color. Gray, brown, and black hats were being replaced with rainbow hues, and "somber black hatbands" were replaced with bands of "riotous color and pattern."[29]

In late 1940, Stetson reported that the British were still shipping coney fur to America as fast as they could, selling fur to pile up dollars for war materials. Stocks of hare skins were still available, but Stetson officials did not expect that to last. Company officials felt they would be alright for a time as they had ten million skins in their Philadelphia factory's basement storage room.[30]

Despite potential war fur shortages, Stetson offered sixty different felt hat styles in 1941 and many summer straw hats "with bands ranging from somber black to most violent Polynesian hues."[31]

Men's hats offered in the 1942-1943 Sears, Roebuck and Company Minneapolis fall and winter catalog, pp. 428B-428C. © 1942-43, Sears, Roebuck and Co.

The offerings for men's western hats in the early 1940s. © 1942-43, Sears, Roebuck and Co.

Sears 1946 men's hats advertised in the Chicago spring and summer catalog, pp. 466-467. © 1946, Sears, Roebuck and Co.

The following are 1940s Stetson advertisements drawn by Philip Dormont of Philadelphia. Philip Dormont was a free-lance artist working with an agent as all part of a studio. The studio charged artists for equipment and materials while the agents drummed up business. Aside from Stetson advertisements, Mr. Dormont penned ads for Swan Soap (the sponsor of the George Burns and Gracie Allen Show), Packard, and Metropolitan Life. His son Paul posed as a sick boy in bed for a Met Life House Call ad. Philip Dormont also put himself in some of his illustrations.

The "Caribou Gray" men's felt Royal Stetson Whippet. This advertisement shows the front of the Stork Club in New York. Philip Dormont knew the owner, Sherman Billingsley and produced a portrait of Dorothy Lamour for him. Celebrities were never charged at the Stork Club and Dormont received the same treatment after creating that portrait. *Life Magazine*. October 29, 1945. p. 94. *Courtesy of Paul Dormont, M.D.*

Royal Stetson Casual men's felt hats in Sunstone color are on display in this ad. The woman's Stetson is called Westminster. *Life Magazine*. April 14, 1946. p. 87. *Courtesy of Paul Dormont, M.D.*

Full page Dormont advertisement for Stetson Hats in front of St. Thomas Church on 5th Avenue and 53rd Street, New York. The narrow brim Stetson men's hat was called Vogue, and is shown in a Chocolate Brown color. The woman's Stetson was called Parade. *Life Magazine*, March 3, 1947. p. 127. *Courtesy of Paul Dormont, M.D.*

Dormont signed all his work. *Courtesy of Paul Dormont, M.D.*

Stetson men's straw hats: left, Stetson Flagship; right, Stetson Warwick. The woman's straw hat was called the Beacon. The location may be Laguardia Airport. *Life Magazine.* May 26, 1947. p. 91. *Courtesy of Paul Dormont, M.D.*

85

A Stetson Casual in Fiesta Oro color is shown. The woman's Stetson is called High Score. *Life Magazine.* April 21, 1947. p. 137. *Courtesy of Paul Dormont, M.D.*

Stetson Flagship box — the airliner is marked AA for American Airlines. *Courtesy of Desire Smith.*

The grey felt Stetson Stratoliner, also of this period, has a small airplane on the ribbon. This is a marvelous old hat. *Courtesy of Patty Stetson.* $150-175

Park Avenue Stetson advertisement: the brown man's Stetson on the left was called The Casual. The woman's Stetson was called Plaza. The gray man's Stetson on the right was called The Whippet. *Life Magazine*. September 8, 1947. p. 14. *Courtesy of Paul Dormont, M.D.*

The felt Stetson on the left is The Campus. The felt Stetson on the right is The Casual. The woman's Stetson is The Mistral. *Life Magazine*. October 6, 1947. p. 10. *Courtesy of Paul Dormont, M.D.*

87

An example of the Royal Stetson Whippet in brown felt and its hat box. The hat is also marked The Bon Marche Northgate, Everett, Seattle. *Courtesy of Patty Stetson.* $75-125

In 1946 Stetson was producing the Royal Stetson and in 1948 the Royal De Luxe Stetson. Note the button beside the hatband bow on the gray Royal Stetson. A cord could be attached to this button and affixed to your lapel to keep your hat from blowing away on windy days. *Courtesy of Patty Stetson.* $75-100 Royal Stetson; $125-150 Royal De Luxe Stetson

The Stetson felt hats shown in this railway station advertisement include: left, men's grey hat, The Flagship; right, men's brown felt hat, The Kashmir. The woman's Stetson was termed the Westport. Life. November 3, 1947. p. 140. *Courtesy of Paul Dormont, M.D.*

1948-1960

By the early 1950s, hat wearing was largely unfashionable. Hat wearers were few and far between and hats never regained their status as fashion statements, except during periods when the odd local craze swept a community. Derbies briefly reappeared in London, for instance.[32]

Dress and western hats offered by Sears in their spring and summer 1949 Los Angeles catalog, p. 344. © 1949, Sears, Roebuck and Co.

The hats of 1951 from the Philadelphia fall and winter Sears catalog, pp. 420-421. You would think that at least in Philadelphia the catalog might have carried a few Stetsons! © 1951, Sears, Roebuck and Co.

1960-1970

An average army officer's peaked cap made famous by the Beatles is the rage for younger men and women alike early in the decade. Unisex clothing is the style. John F. Kennedy reinforces men's desire to remain barehded. Cowboy and homesteader hats with broad brims are popular casual wear, warming the hearts of everyone at Stetson.[33]

Harry Platt, the president of Local 60, United Hatters, Cap & Millinery Workers International Union at Stetson complained that the introduction of the cloth "Rex Harrison" style hat in the 1960s "was killing" his felt hat industry. "The felt hat industry has deteriorated so much it's pitiful." Platt said. He added that Stetson had moved into the sporty cloth hat market, but that the company did not manufacture its own cloth hats. Those were manufactured in Stetson's Canadian branch factory.[34]

Very few hats for men (or women) were offered in 1970. These two hats are from the 1970 Sears Chicago fall and winter catalog, pp. 706-707. Seeing these, it is obvious that the Stetson Company would not be able to sell enough quality hats to stay in business in Philadelphia. © 1970, Sears, Roebuck and Co.

The 1960 fall and winter hat offerings for men from the Sears Seattle catalog, pp. 674-675. © 1960, Sears, Roebuck and Co.

An article in which Harry Platt discusses the decline in the hat industry and one of his business cards. According to Irene Centofanti, the Stetson Company's business was in serious decline by 1961. *Courtesy of Irene Centofanti.*

1970-1980

As Stetson closed the doors on their Philadelphia plant, a back-to-your-roots ethnic movement was bringing patchwork hats and berets festooned with sequins and embroidery into fashion. Felt hats became pop music symbols. Stetson's licensee, the Stetson Hat Group would focus primarily on western hats.[35]

1980-1990s

The movies bring back another fedora when Harrison Ford dons his as the swashbuckling archaeologist Indiana Jones in *Raiders of the Lost Ark*. This would be a big seller for the licensee carrying the Stetson brand name into the future in 1984. Western hats continue to be manufactured, protecting men from weather and making fashion statements wherever they appear. The single most common hat of the 1990s is probably the cloth baseball cap.

Western Stetsons, The Company's Staple Hats

Stetson's western hats are extremely difficult to date with any degree of accuracy. The styles changed slowly and the hats were worn for many years. Another frustration associated with Stetson's western hats is that while they are given names in catalogs, the hats themselves rarely, if ever, carry these names in the sweatbands or linings. What follows is a photo gallery with a sampling of some of the wonderful western hats Stetson produced over many decades. This Montana Peak crown, No. 1 Quality, stiff flat brimmed, raw edged hat goes way back. The style was popular in the 1890s and is similar to examples offered by the company in 1910. It has a 5 1/2" high crown and 3" wide brim. *Courtesy of Bruce Mackinnon.* $100-125

No. 50. Burros Loaded with Deer.—D. B. Chase, Photographer, Santa Fe, N. M.

Courtesy of Lynn Trusdell.

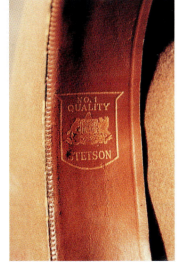

A No. 1 Quality unlined Stetson with a bound brim. The sweatband is stamp with a retailer's name and location: Hamley & Co., Pendleton, Oregon. *Courtesy of Elmer and Jan Diederich.* $100-150

A telescope crown, No. 1 Quality, unlined Stetson with a bound brim. The retailer's name and location, Wilson-Foster Inc. of Lompoc, California, is printed in the sweatband. Stetson opened an office in California in the early 1920s. *Courtesy of Elmer and Jan Diederich.* $125-150

A 3X Beaver Quality unlined Stetson with a bound brim. *Courtesy of Elmer and Jan Diederich.*

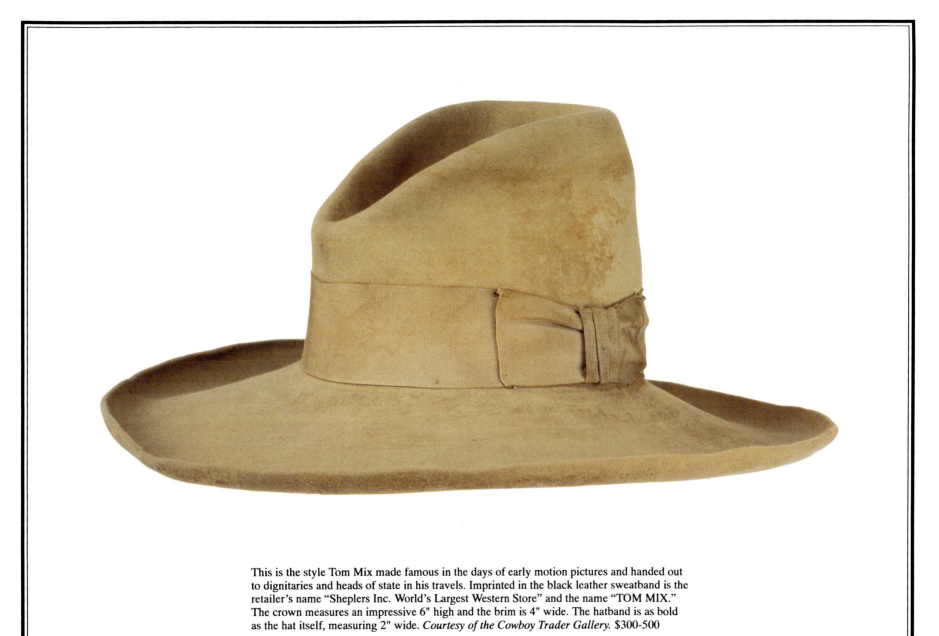

This is the style Tom Mix made famous in the days of early motion pictures and handed out to dignitaries and heads of state in his travels. Imprinted in the black leather sweatband is the retailer's name "Sheplers Inc. World's Largest Western Store" and the name "TOM MIX." The crown measures an impressive 6" high and the brim is 4" wide. The hatband is as bold as the hat itself, measuring 2" wide. *Courtesy of the Cowboy Trader Gallery.* $300-500

A white No. 1 Quality staple hat with a pencil roll brim. There is no silk lining. It is similar in size and scale to the Tom Mix hat. 6" high crown, 3 1/2" wide brim. *Courtesy of Ray Huffman, Broken Heart Trading.* $300-400

Next Page:
A bold white Stetson with matching hat band and binding. *Courtesy of Dick Engel.* $500-700

A beautiful Stetson Number 1 Quality hat with a 5" kettle curl brim and a 7" crown. *Courtesy of Dick Engel.* $500-700

Stetson No. 1 Quality stamp in the sweatband leather. *Courtesy of Dick Engel.*

This early Stetson, with its matching hatband and binding, has seen a lot of use. There is no sweatband left. It features a high 7 1/2" crown with a forward dipping crease and an equally wide 7 1/2" brim. *Courtesy of Dick Engel.* $400-500

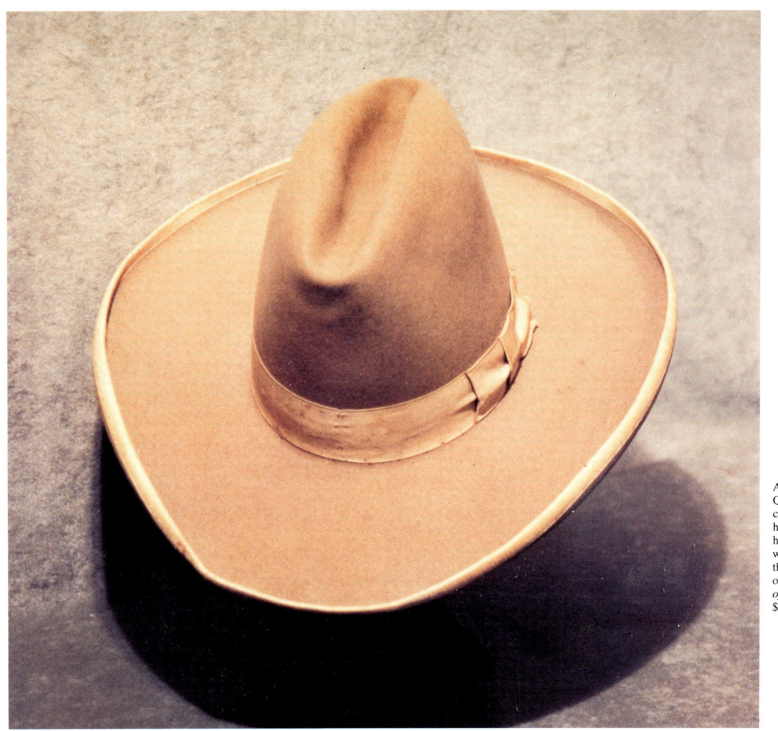

100

An oval crowned, No. 1 Quality Stetson with a long central crease and matching hatband and binding. This hat is lined and imprinted with "The Denver." Could this be an actual hat name on a western hat? *Courtesy of Elmer and Jan Diederich.* $300-500

A broad, raw-edge-brimmed Stetson with an oval crown and a forward dipping central crease which was made for Hamley & Co. of Pendleton, Oregon. This hat has been nicely trimmed with a striking band. *Courtesy of Elmer and Jan Diederich.* $300-500

This hat is similar to the Montana Special illustrated in the 1928 Stockman-Farmer Supply Company catalog. It has a raw edge, 6" brim and a 7 1/2" high dome crown. *Courtesy of the collection of Larry and Marylin Robinson.* $600-800

A very fine high dome crown clear nutria white Stetson with a brilliant red lining. The lining itself is marked "Made Expressly for Max J. Meyer Co. Inc., Cheyenne." The crown is 7 1/2" high and the brim is 5" wide. A big man wearing this hat was sure to attract attention. *Courtesy of the collection of Charlie and Karla Smith.* $600-800

Another fine high dome crown clear nutria white Stetson western hat. The binding is secured along the exposed outer edge of the brim and is made of the same grosgrain material as the hatband. The sweatband is marked "Bond Bros. Pendleton, Oregon" and also carries the famous "Let 'Er Buck Pendleton Round-Up" mark. The crown is 6 1/2" high and the brim is 4" wide. *Courtesy of the collection of Charlie and Karla Smith.* $600-800

103

Stetson Number 1 Quality Western marked "A L Furstnow," a famous saddle mark from Miles City, Montana. Brim size 4", crown 6". *Courtesy of Dick Engel.* $200-400

A great nutria fur Stetson with a rare Pendleton Roundup distributor's mark. *Courtesy of Dick Engel.* $300-500

Stetson's "Made of Real Nutria Fur" mark for quality soft hats. In 1901, Stetsons with this mark sold for $48.00 per dozen or more. *Courtesy of Dick Engel.*

This Stetson is marked "Made of Real Nutria Fur" and was produced for a store in Casper, Wyoming. The crown measures 7" and the brim measures 7 1/2". *Courtesy of Dick Engel.* $200-400

A marvelous, raw-edged, broad-brimmed Stetson — the brim measures 7 1/2" and the crown is 7". *Courtesy of Dick Engel.* $500-700

This Stetson shows signs of hard use, especially along the brim binding. It has a striking band. The crown and brim both measure 7 1/2". *Courtesy of Dick Engel.* $500-700

A 4X Beaver felt western hat in the short, stockman style with a curled brim. It has a lining adorned with "The Last Drop From His Stetson." The crown measures 4 1/2" high; the brim measures 2 3/4" wide. *Courtesy of W.D. Clarke.* $150-250

The boy wishing to emulate his father could wear a small version of the short, stockman style hat called the "Stetson Junior Cowboy." This example is marked "G. Fox & Co. Est. 1847 Hartford" in the sweatband. It has a 4 1/2" crown and a 2 3/4" brim. *Courtesy of Bruce Mackinnon.* $100-200

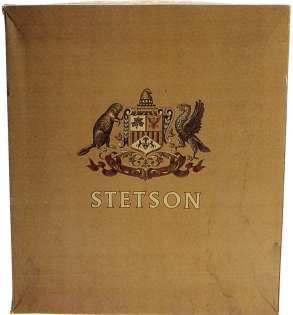

An Open Road tan Stetson and the box it rode in on. This was the favorite of American presidents from the 1940s through the 1960s. The Open Road measures 4 1/2" high at the crown and 2 1/2" wide at the brim. A grosgrain hat band and binding finishes the hat. This square box style was in general use by Stetson in the 1960s. *Courtesy of the author's collection.* $200-300

A 4X Beaver raw edge brim hat with a 3 1/4" brim and a 5 1/4" high crown. *Courtesy of Lynn Trusdell.* $200-300

A 4X Beaver raw edge brim Stetson with a braided band, a 3 3/4" wide brim, and a 5 1/4" high crown. *Courtesy of Lynn Trusdell.* $200-300

An "Appaloosa" natural straw western hat by Stetson. It has a 5" high crown and a 3 1/2" wide brim. *Courtesy of W.D. Clarke.* $75-100

An open weave natural straw "Roadrunner" hat. A cool summer Stetson with a 5" high crown and a 4" wide brim. *Courtesy of the author's collection.* $75-100

These last three western Stetsons were all made after 1970. This was one of the hats produced by the Stetson Group. The lining features the image "The Last Drop From His Stetson" in full color. *Courtesy of Joy Shih Ng.* $75-100

This post-1970 3X Beaver hat with a raw edge brim has seen a lot of hard wear. Its lining also features "The Last Drop From His Stetson." *Courtesy of Richard Whiteford.* $50-90

A post-1970 4X Beaver felt western hat with a telescope crown, a raw edge brim, and a finely tooled leather hatband. Again, the lining is adorned with "The Last Drop From His Stetson." The crown measures 4 1/2" high and the brim measures 3" wide. *Courtesy of James J. Snyder.* $75-125

A formidable large blue-black, modern 4X Beaver Stetson western hat.
Courtesy of Charlie Lee, Annville, Pennsylvania. $400-600

Stetson Dress Hats

A 1920s Stetson Premier Panama straw hat with a navy blue hatband that is marked "Stetson Premier. Genuine Panama" on the sweatband. It is also marked with the owner's initials "FAR" and the retailer's name "The Carlson Company."
Courtesy of Joan Palicia. $75-100

This Stetson Twenty fedora with a wind catcher button on side is lined and was sold at the 1224 Chestnut Street shop in Philadelphia. *Courtesy of John J. Twers.* $75-100

A gray Royal Stetson felt fedora with a bold, black hatband. *Courtesy of Patty Stetson.* $75-100

124

A classic example of a Stetson snap brim hat. *Courtesy of Patty Stetson.* $75-125

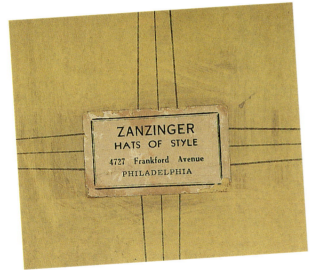

This Stetson Premier gray felt hat was marked "Vita Felt Process." It is a very soft hat with a wide black band. It was found in this yellow oval hat box marked "Zanninger House of Style," a Philadelphia firm. *Courtesy of Desire Smith.* $100-125 hat.

A black Royal Stetson snap brim hat with a wide band, the only hat style Frank Sinatra ever wore. Sammy Davis Jr. wore them too. *Courtesy of John J. Twers.* $75-125

This black felt Royal Stetson hat has a wide hatband embellished with a feather. *Courtesy of Joan Palicia.* $75-125

128

This is a gray felt Royal DeLuxe Stetson, with a telescope crown and a very narrow brim, dubbed "The Gun Club." *Courtesy of Irene Centofanti.* $75-100

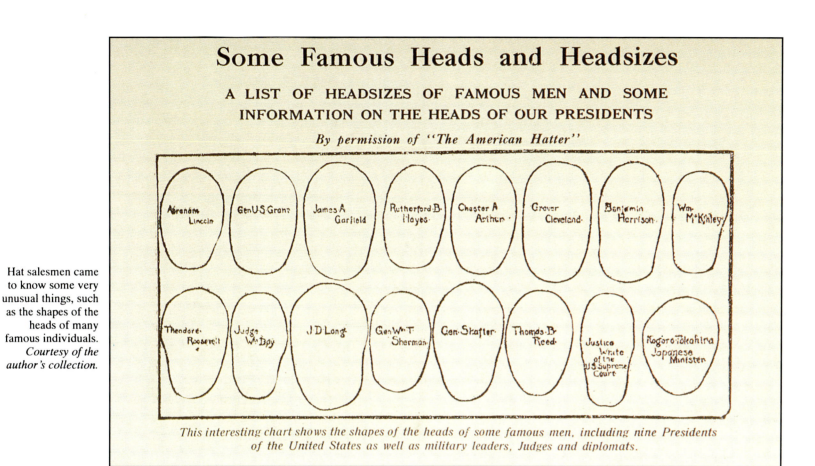

Hat salesmen came to know some very unusual things, such as the shapes of the heads of many famous individuals. *Courtesy of the author's collection.*

129

Hat Etiquette For Men

When John B. Stetson began manufacturing hats in earnest in 1865, a hat was not just plopped on the head and forgotten. How the hat was worn, what hat went with which clothing, when a hat was removed, and even what messages the wearer wished to send by the tilt of that hat were matters of serious concern. As these are virtually hatless times in America, it is best to brush up on the dos and don't of hat etiquette before venturing out in any newly acquired Stetsons. While you are less likely to commit a social faux pas with your Stetson at the rodeo than on Rodeo Drive, most of these regulations can be safely applied to western and dress hats alike.

When to "Doff"

When and how to remove a hat in a particular circumstance was of keen importance to nineteenth century men-about-town. Doffing was, and remains, a sign of respect and humility. Nineteenth century books and articles set aside a lot of space to discuss the intricacies of doffing.

In 1882 the *Collier's Cyclopedia of Commercial and Social Information* provided the following insights:[36]

On the street ladies bow first to a gentleman and a gentleman so saluted lifts his hat and bows. When a gentleman leaves a ladies company, he also lifts his hat.

According to what Stetson salesmen inferred about customers by the tilt of their hats when they entered the shop, Doug Fairbanks, Jr. loved the "delicately intimated" compliment. *Courtesy of the author's collection.*

A simple start, but things get a little more complicated, taxing coordination. On the matter of opening doors, gentlemen open "store, and all other doors for ladies to pass, lifting his hat at the same time."

Please remove your hat and observe a moment of silence before we continue. At funerals, unless you are a pall bearer, hats must be removed as the coffin passes from the hearse to the church, and from the church to the hearse.

Everyone knows that the first thing a cowboy put on in the morning and the last thing he took off at night was his hat. However, every cowpoke, city slicker, and suburbanite must leave the hat, coat, umbrella, cane, and overshoes in the hall when on an informal evening call.

Those are the simple, straight forward rules of the game. However, nothing was ever simple in Victorian society. A nineteenth century gentleman would not feel the need to remove his hat when stepping into his butcher's shop. The butcher was a merchant and a merchant was a tradesperson requiring no such display of respect. However, the banker was a professional, worthy of a gentleman's tip of the hat.[37]

By the 1890s, men were getting a little weary trying to remember which fellow deserved the doff. The rules changed and almost every man viewed a mere touch of the hand to the brim as an adequate sign of respect.[38]

In 1940, men were advised that it was polite to take a hat off when they were on elevators with ladies.

Hard and fast rules which never change when wearing a western Stetson included always removing your hat when entering someone's home. Business establishments do not count, only living spaces. Also, always remove your hat when first meeting a lady. On subsequent meetings, tip your hat to her. Remember who you have met, gentlemen![39]

The Hat, Character, and Class

The type of hat someone chose to wear and how they wore it spoke volumes to the trained eye. Poke bonnets and mob caps were popular among unmarried or widowed Victorian women long after married women and girls gave them up for other fashions. Victorian men had to be very careful not to wear the wrong hat with a particular suit. The bowler (derby or "pot hat") was not to be worn with a frock coat (morning coat). Only the top hat would do for such formal attire. However, after World War I, this particular mandate was shattered on Wall Street and bowlers proliferated as proper power suit attire.[40]

It is time to name names. Mashers wore little hats on rigidly held heads, gave stony stares, forced the hat straight up almost to arms length and straight down again in the doff, and carried big canes. Hat snappers were swells who removed hats and snapped them down suddenly to the waist, holding them upside down. Dignified gentlemen, on the other hand, lifted the hat at an angle, inclined the head forward graciously, and avoided all swagger. Make your choice when doffing your Stetson.[41]

What the Stetson Salesman Saw[42]

In 1924, Stetson salesmen also sized men up by the way the wore their hats when entering the shop. Their measure was a little different. If a man wore his hat tilted sharply down to the eyes he was a "penetrative thinker," needing less sales pitch and more time in front of the mirror. He was methodical, uncommunicative, and could not be hurried, but was reasonable and reasoning. "This kind of man is not sold a hat, he buys the hat."

The man who wore his hat tilted sharply down to the right loved the compliment if "delicately intimated." The sales pitch was to be geared to vanity. Such a man liked light colors and was self-opinionated, but was also responsive to suggestion. "This man is easily raised to higher priced-goods with properly directed sales arguments." To put it more bluntly, this sort of man was vain and gullible.

A man who wore his hat straight on was most often middle-aged, settled, conservative, of good stock, reasoning, and agreeable. Basically, this was a dull guy. However, he was a careful buyer who considered price and quality as well as style. He was considered a dependable prospect as a repeat customer.

The man who wore his hat sharply tilted back up off his forehead was self-confident and had his own ideas of what he wanted. He did not take advice and was usually not a good judge of proper style. He did not have particularly good taste in clothes, liked to be "solicitously handled," and could be convinced of almost anything provided he thought it was his own idea.

Finally, if a man entered the shop with his hat sloped from front to back and tight down over his ears, the salesman knew to watch out. This was an extremely confident, obstinate, and unyielding man. The salesman could pitch a style or a quality until he was blue in the face and this fellow would still sacrifice both for a cheap price. He was identified as a "close buyer; he makes the best possible test for sales brilliance."

Beware of the "Jape"

Miscreants and idlers about town in America in the late nineteenth century were fond of "playing the jape." They slipped a particularly strong smelling sliver of cheese under a friend's sweatband and watched the fun when the unsuspecting victim traveled home in a crowded tramcar on a hot summer's night. The smell of a well used summer sweatband could be bad enough, but this would have been intolerable. Best to keep your Stetson close at hand when mingling at a wine and cheese party.[43]

Chapter IV

Women's Hats

Stetson produced women's hats for "outdoor recreations" during the late 1800s. Of course, nothing stopped women from wearing men's western hats, as photographs from Buffalo Bill's Wild West Show prove. By the 1930s, Stetson's company had opened its own millinery department within the sprawling complex, manufacturing dress hats for two decades. Stetson ceased its millinery production in the early 1950s.

Women's Hats From 1870-1920

1870-1900

Fashionable women with money to spend invested small fortunes on their clothing and accessories. Wealthy women with a penchant for conspicuous consumption spent many hours every week with dressmakers and milliners. Hats adorned with feathers of every shape, size, and color conveyed considerable status to the women wearing them.

Hats had gone out of fashion in the 1860s and were returning in the 1870s. In the early 1870s, hats as informal headwear became popular. Wide-brimmed bergeres and straw sailor hats were all fashionable. Small Tyrolean velvet and silk hats with little turned up brims were considered a little racy and most women preferred a more staid Glengarry or pork-pie hat.[1]

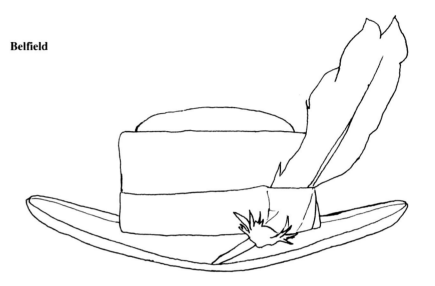

Belfield

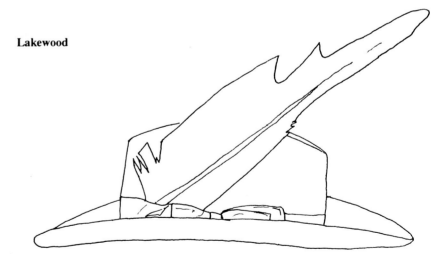

Lakewood

Ladies hats offered by Stetson in 1899 for "participating in any of the numerous field sports which women now indulge in." The top hat is titled Belfield and the lower hat is called Lakewood.

During the decade of the 1870s, women's hat styles multiply. The Dolly Varden was very popular, worn with a very wide brim and a flat crown. Basic bonnet variations were everywhere. Charlotte Corday, Capote, and toques were all popular. By the late 1890s, both homburg and flower pot hats were very fashionable. Hats were increasingly trimmed with feathers as a status symbol and the most fashionable hats required a veil.[2]

In 1899, the Stetson Monthly illustrated two ladies' hats, the Belfield and the Lakewood, both with a large feather tucked into the band. These felt hats were described as "... the proper thing to match the tailor-made gown, for morning wear and when participating in any of the numerous field sports which women now indulge in." The Belfield had a 5" high crown and 3 1/4" wide brim. The Lakewood measured 4 1/4" high at the crown and 3" wide at the brim.[3]

1900-1920

Women's hats begin small at the start of the century and explode in scale by the end of this period. In 1900, a small hat with a little veil resting gently on the head is all the rage in Paris, London, and New York and is at its best in black. By 1910, size is the thing, most women's hats are very large indeed.[4]

Scale, provided by hat trims, is considered quite important in all social spheres. Artificial flowers, feathers, tulle, and waxed satin ribbons bloom with exuberance on ladies hats. Toques are popular if worn tilted back off the face. By 1914, the sheer number and varieties of hat styles rivals those of the late nineteenth century.[5]

The Stetson Company would not enter the women's millinery market until c. 1930.

The Stetson Company began producing women's hats in 1930. For the Spring of 1932, this Doondale Cheviot beret was among the offerings. *Courtesy of The Atwater Kent Museum.*

Women's Hats From 1920 Onward

1920-1930

The cloche hat became the most fashionable woman's hat of the 1920, for young and old alike. Broader brimmed "picture" hats were frequently worn in the summer for outdoor activities.[6]

1930-1939

Wide brimmed hats replace the cloche hats during the early 1930s. By the mid-1930s, high hats of modest size based on the Tyrol, the sailor's hat, and the fez are common. Also fashionable by mid-decade were berets, pillboxes, and tricornes. By the end of the decade the slouch hat, worn with the brim over one eye, is a hit along with high, often pointed, crowned hats. Turbans, hoods, and snoods were popular by 1939 and would remain in style throughout World War II. Stetson begins producing women's dress hats during this decade at the Philadelphia plant.[7]

A rare 1930s yellow, wide-brimmed felt fedora featuring two blue stars on the grosgrain hatband. Inside the band, the hat is marked with a circular Stetson mark and the phrase "Made Exclusively For John Wanamaker Philadelphia." A small elastic string inside the hat helped to hold it on when hidden under a woman's hair in back. *Courtesy of Desire Smith.* $65-85

As with the men's hats, none of the hats advertised in the Sears catalogs are Stetsons. They are, however, of the same styles offered by Stetson and are useful to help pin individual hat styles down to particular decade or to several decades. Women's hats offered in the 1938-39 Sears, Roebuck and Company Boston catalog for the fall and winter, pp. 97-107. © 1938-39, Sears, Roebuck and Co.

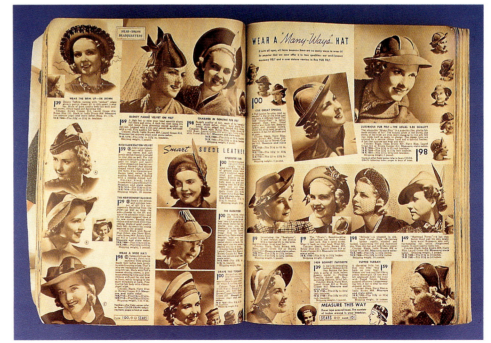

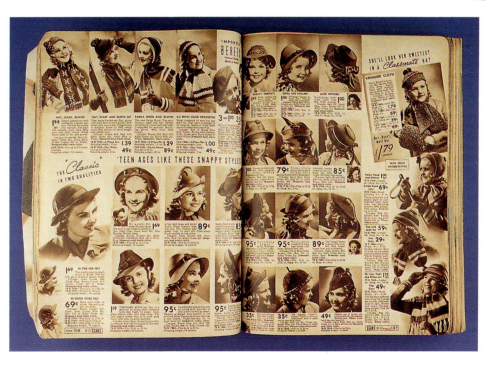

A 1930s doll hat covered with aqua and black ostrich feathers. This hat has a tiny net veil in black. Two labels are sewn together inside the hat, giving the locations of the Philadelphia and New York Stetson shops: "STETSON HAT SHOP 1224 CHESTNUT STREET PHILADELPHIA" and "STETSON FIFTH AVENUE." *Donated by Desire Smith to The Atwater Kent Museum.* NP

Freedom Fashions by STETSON

HATTERS' HIGHLIGHTS

In 1943 Dorothy Lamour, Carole Landis and Susan Hayward collaborated with Stetson Hats, Inc., in featuring Stetson hats for women, and most successfully, too. They were shown, each wearing three different styles, grouped under the designation "Freedom Fashions" illustrated in national magazines.

The idea of selecting certain styles sponsored by motion picture stars known to the world, not only for their fine acting in Paramount Pictures, but for their good taste in dress, met with the hearty approval of the stores selling Stetson hats, whose sales increased materially.

Now for Spring of 1944, four other popular Paramount actresses are being pictured in the magazines—Life, Mademoiselle, Vogue and Town and Country. They are Betty Hutton, Barbara Britton, Veronica Lake and Gail Russell, each in three styles, twelve hats in all, and the four words, "Freedom Fashions by Stetson" are growing to greater importance among women who keep in touch with the developments of new style ideas.

The selection of styles includes hats to be worn "round-the-clock"—morning, afternoon or evening for a dinner date—casuals for country wear, and modified berets.

They are being featured by dealers in special window displays, newspaper advertisements and by mail with a folder illustrating the new styles.

BARBARA BRITTON — "The Benning"
BETTY HUTTON — "The Montezuma"
BETTY HUTTON — "The Pensacola"

"The Corsair" GAIL RUSSELL
"The Corvette" BARBARA BRITTON
"The Musette" BETTY HUTTON
"The Echelon" VERONICA LAKE
GAIL RUSSELL "The Guardsman"

Some of Stetson's 1944 spring "Freedom Fashions" for women. *Courtesy of Irene Centofanti.*

1940-1945

In 1940, Paris fell, cutting off the source of many fashion changes, and lead to the repetition of 1930s styles. During the 1940s, turbans were standard for working women in British and North American factories retooled for war. Military hats influenced women's hat designs as well, leading to many peaked-caps. These were very similar to those worn by soldiers. Stetson moves its millinery department to New York in c. 1941, where it will remain for a decade.[8]

Women's hats offered in the 1942-43 Sears, Roebuck and Company Minneapolis fall and winter catalog, pp. 104-114. If you look closely, you will find several styles based on men's dress and military hats. © 1942-43, Sears, Roebuck and Co.

1946-1960

In the 1950s, hair styles limit hat wearing. However, hats linger longer as fashion statements in the women's market than in the men's. Hat styles for the 1950s are either very small, such as flat pancake berets and pillboxes, or very large, including romantic picture hats harkening back to turn-of-the-century styles. The Coolie hat becomes a fashion to emulate, copied in cheap, stiff straw hats.[9]

A 1940s brown felt beret marked "Stetson Mistral." An elastic band inside the beret was provided to help keep the hat in place on windy days. This hat appears in the October 6, 1947 *Life Magazine* Stetson advertisement. *Courtesy of Patty Stetson.* $45-50

A 1950s white dyed straw picture hat with a red and white polka-dot band and white cloth flowers. It is labeled "John B. Stetson." *Courtesy of Desire Smith.* $85-125

A 1940s wide-brimmed natural straw with a pale green grosgrain band bearing a Stetson Fifth Avenue label. *Courtesy of Desire Smith.* $95-150

A 1940s natural straw with a brown grosgrain band. The hat is labeled Stetson Fifth Avenue and Claire Hat Store/Pottstown, Pa. *Courtesy of Desire Smith.* $60-75

148

A 1940s natural straw with a green grosgrain band. It is also labeled Stetson Fifth Avenue and Claire Hat Shop/Pottstown Pa. *Courtesy of Desire Smith.* $60-75

A dark blue felt hat with a broad grosgrain band and a cord running through the crown, marked "Stetson Fifth Avenue. Boust & Stahl Sunbury, Pa." *Courtesy of Patty Stetson.* $45-55

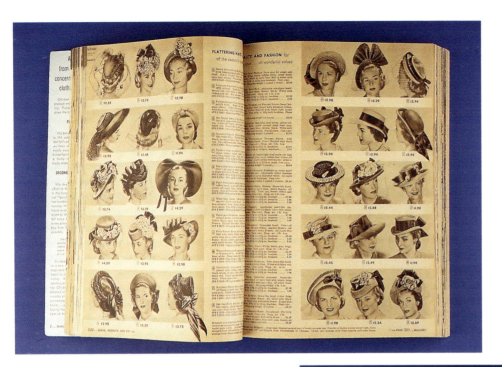

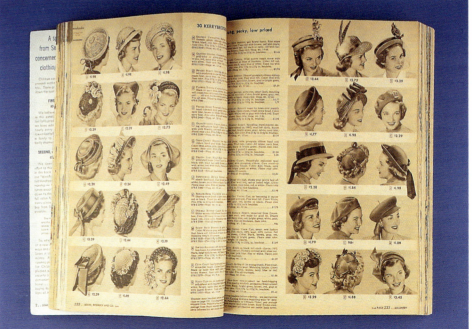

The 1949 women's hats advertised in the spring and summer Sears Los Angeles catalog, pp. 220-223. © 1949, Sears, Roebuck and Co.

These are the hats Sears was offering in 1951 in the Philadelphia fall and winter Sears catalog, pp. 274-279. © 1951, Sears, Roebuck and Co.

151

152

A dark blue felt hat with a broad band, marked "Stetson Fifth Avenue" and "John Wanamaker." *Courtesy of Patty Stetson.* $45-55

A black, square crowned felt hat with a wide grosgrain band and binding, marked "Stetson Hat Shop/1224 Chestnut Street/Philadelphia" and "Stetson Fifth Avenue." *Courtesy of Patty Stetson.* $45-55

154

A 1950s blue wide brim with white lace flowers and rhinestones, labeled "Stetson Fifth Avenue. John B. Stetson Company." *Courtesy of Patty Stetson.* $50-60

A 1950s white wide brim velour with two rhinestone pins decorating the band. *Courtesy of Patty Stetson.* $65-70

156

A small 1950s brown wide brimmed felt hat with a large feather around the brim, marked "Stetson Fifth Avenue" and "Bzannstein's The Fashion Capital of Delaware." *Courtesy of Patty Stetson.* $55-65

A brown circular felt hat with bead work around the band and brown netting to draw down over face. An elastic string was provided to hold the hat in place on windy days. The hat is labeled "Stetson Fifth Avenue." *Courtesy of Desire Smith.* $65-85

A 1950s black felt clip with silver bead decoration, labeled "Stetson. 1224 Chestnut Street. Philadelphia" and "Aurora. Made in France." The felt is French. *Courtesy of Patty Stetson.* $45-50

A 1950s black felt with two silk feathers decorated with glass beads, labeled "Stetson. 1224 Chestnut Street. Philadelphia." *Courtesy of Desire Smith.* $65-80

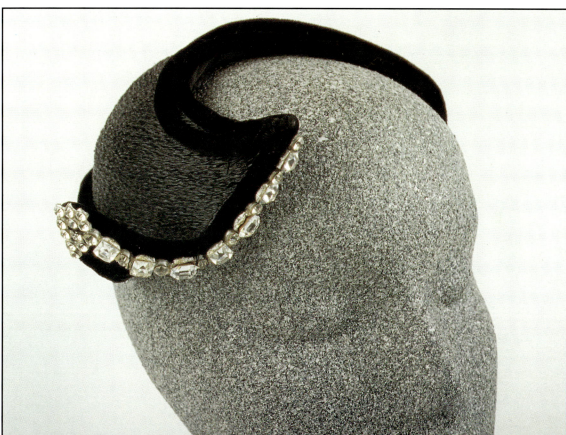

A 1950s black straw bodied clip hat decorated with rhinestones, labeled "Stetson. 1224 Chestnut Street. Philadelphia." *Courtesy of Patty Stetson.* $45-50

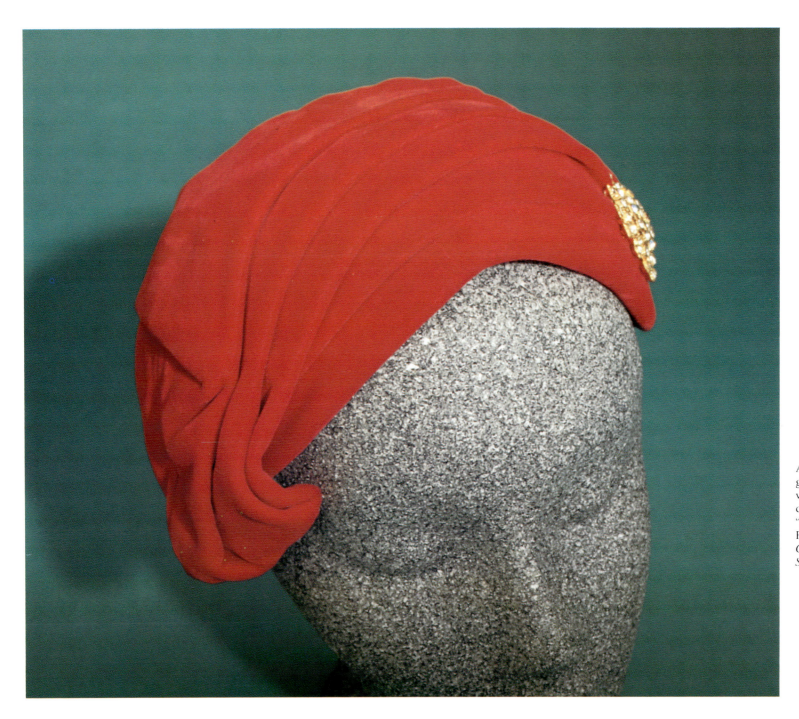

160

A 1950s red gathered velveteen with rhinestone decoration, labeled "John B. Stetson Fifth Avenue." *Courtesy of Desire Smith.* $65-85

161

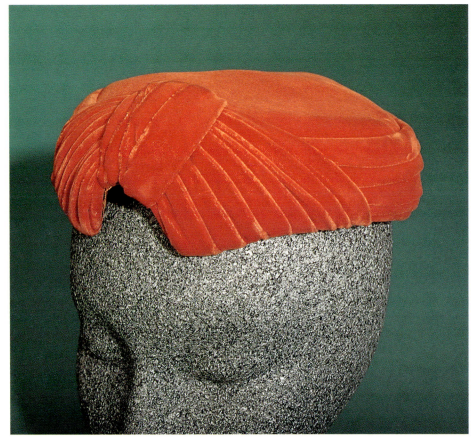

162

A 1950s orange velveteen cocktail hat, labeled "Stetson. 1224 Chestnut Street. Philadelphia." *Courtesy of Desire Smith.* $65-85

A 1950s pink felt covered with silver glass beads, salmon colored sequins, and a veil. It is labeled, "Stetson. 1224 Chestnut Street. Philadelphia." *Donated by Desire Smith to The Atwater Kent Museum.* NP

A 1950s orange and green velveteen decorated with crossed rhinestones. This hat is lined with a multicolored leaf-patterned material and is labeled, "Made Expressly For John B. Stetson Company Fifth Ave. New York." *Courtesy of Desire Smith.* $65-85

165

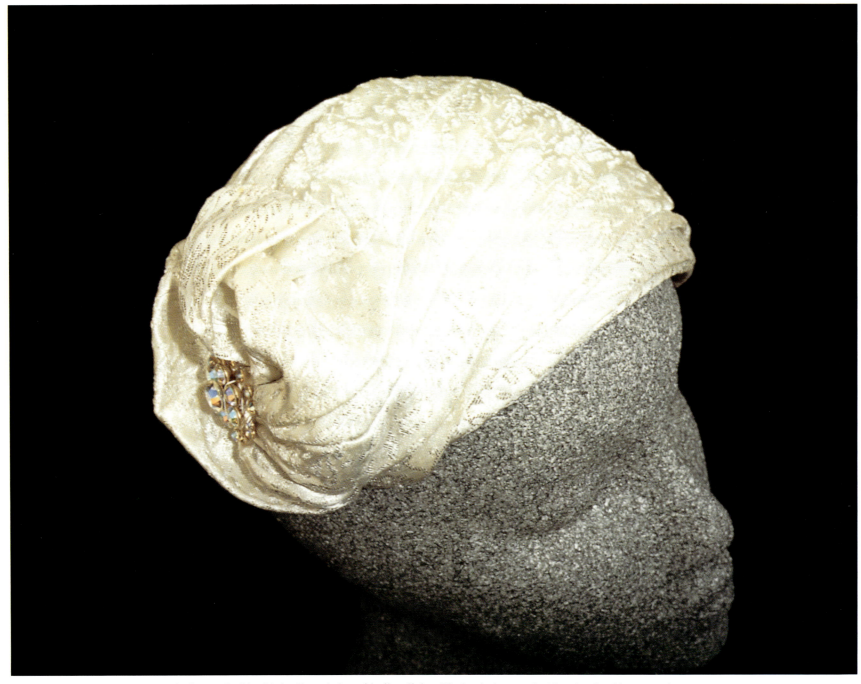

A silver and white fabric clip style hat with silver lining. The hat is decorated with a circular rhinestone piece in the center of a fabric flower. This hat is labeled, "Stetson Fifth Avenue." *Courtesy of Desire Smith.* $65-85

167

A 1950s white floral over net with a green veil over the flowers. It is labeled, "Stetson. 1224 Chestnut Street. Philadelphia" and "Emme Boutique." Emme was a big name in women's fashions. *Courtesy of Desire Smith.* $55-80

A 1950s miniature floral over net with an overriding green veil, labeled "Stetson. 1224 Chestnut Street. Phila." *Courtesy of Desire Smith.* $50-75

Black felt hat with a gold interior lining and circular rhinestone decoration on one side, labeled "Stetson Fifth Avenue." *Courtesy of Desire Smith.* $65-85

A green hat with orange and brown silk trim and tassels, marked "Stetson. All Silk Hand Slip Stretched. John B. Stetson Company." *Courtesy of Patty Stetson.* $65-75

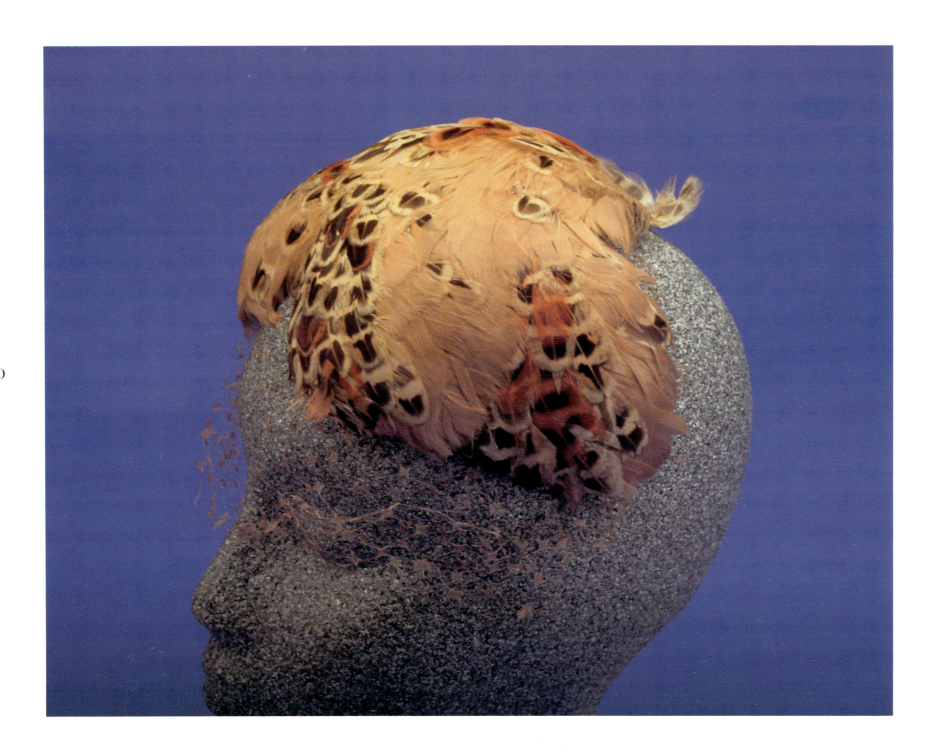

An unlabeled feathered ladies Stetson with netting. The hat has a brown lining and an adjustable band to affix the hat to the head. Collectors should snap these feathered hats up when they can. Men consider them very good raw material for fishing lures. *Courtesy of Peggy A. DeAngelo.* $55-60

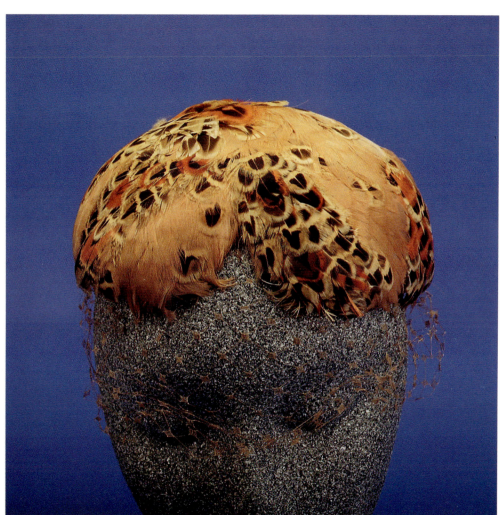

1960-1970

As with men, the average army officer's peaked cap made famous by the Beatles is the rage for younger women early in the decade. Unisex clothing is the style. Jacqueline Kennedy strengthens the popularity of the pillbox for women. Oversized toques of wolf, fox, and imitation fur called "Doctor Zhivago" hats become the glamour statement for women. Cowboy and homesteader hats with broad brims are popular casual wear, warming the hearts of everyone at Stetson. Piratical handkerchiefs and scarves pulled across the forehead also gain a following. In the waning years of the decade, soft, "romantic" pull-on hats in a knitted anti-fashion form gain favor.[10]

The 1960 catalog offerings are getting sparse. A few retro designs are to be found in the Sears Seattle catalog, pp. 140-143. © 1960, Sears, Roebuck and Co.

As with men's hats, by 1970 there was very little to be found in the catalog in the way of women's millinery. These hats were advertised in the Sears Chicago fall and winter catalog, p. 312. © 1970, Sears, Roebuck and Co.

1970-1980

As Stetson closed the doors on their Philadelphia plant, a back-to-your-roots ethnic movement was bringing patchwork hats and berets festooned with sequins and embroidery into fashion. Soft, tweed, pull-on styles based on *Annie Hall* became popular by the closing years of the decade. Milliners revamped the fedora for women, establishing a "retro" look which included 1920s cloche and 1930s slouch hats. Knitted, crocheted, and felt hats were also popular. Stetson's licensee, the Stetson Hat Group would focus primarily on western hats, worn by men and women alike.[11]

1980-1990s

Western hats continue to be manufactured, protecting women from the weather and making fashion statements wherever they appear.

In the 1990s, women have caught up with men, almost entirely forsaking hats. Informal attire, fast-paced business and family lives, lower and sleeker car styles, and a continued emphasis on hair styles over head wear have driven all but the most utilitarian rain hats, hoods, and caps from the heads of men and women alike.[12]

Chapter V

Care of Hats

Searching For and Evaluating Hats

There are many vintage hats to be found on the market today. Difficulty arises when seeking older hats, especially pre-1900 western Stetsons. These hats were subject to much hard wear and all sorts of weather. When found they tend to show a lot of "character" and are a treasure. Hats with the names of famous distributors or well known owners printed in the bands are particularly fine prizes.[1]

Hats may be searched for in many places. Instead of waiting for the highway crew or marine archaeologists to turn up remarkably preserved hats, check estate, yard, and tag sales, flea markets, thrift shops, auctions, and dealers. Also, carefully check advertisements under the headings "Clothing Bought and Sold," and "Vintage, Secondhand, or Used Clothing" in the yellow pages.[2]

Examine hats carefully before buying them. With the exception of stiff hats, felt should remain pliable. Avoid dried out material. Look for cracks in stiff hats. Hold woven straw hats up to the light and look for patches, knots, and holes.[3]

Check a hats color, if it has faded, it has also lost its flexibility. Lightly pinch the brim, it should bend easily and not crackle or crunch.[4]

There are many marvelous vintage Stetsons out there waiting to be found by those who are up to the search. This is a handsome dark blue clear nutria felt Stetson western hat, labeled "John B. Stetson Co. Phila. Waterproof."
Courtesy of The Atwater Kent Museum. NP

When looking for women's millinery, check the cloth labels. Better quality hats usually carried two labels, one from the store and the other from the manufacturer. The better stores carried the finest quality hats.[5]

When looking at labels or seeking the printed trademarks in sweatbands, remember that local hat shops were often equipped to renovate battered, time worn head wear. Shops servicing Stetsons (and this probably applies to other brands as well) had blocks for reshaping and could replace sweatbands and linings. When sweatbands and linings were replaced, the original labels and trademarks were lost. If a hat does not have a label or mark it does not necessarily mean it is not a Stetson, it may be a renovated Stetson.[6]

Caring for Hats

When dealing with vintage hats, purists never wear them, less strict collectors wear them when their hair is very clean, and nobody takes the aging hat out in a downpour. Stiff hats will lose their glue and stiffening in the rain. Straw hats will collapse. Keep a close eye on the weather when wearing vintage hats. If you are caught in the rain with your felt hat, turn out the sweatband to dry it and to provide a platform for the hat to slowly dry on. Gently push out the creases and dents to make the crown as rounded as possible. Never use a hair dryer as this will wrinkle and damage the hat. Once the hat is dry, gently reform the creases.[7]

Whether vintage or modern, dust your hat daily with a soft-bristled brush. Stiff bristled brushes will tear the felt. Western stores frequently sell hatter's brushes for this dusting job. Use a dark colored brush for dark hats and a light colored brush for light hats.[8]

A damp towel with a slight nap can also be used to remove dust. Gently rub the dampened towel in a circular counterclockwise motion over the surface to quickly remove dust. A soft towel used to dry off with after a shower will work. Remember, do not try this with a stiff hat, moist shellac is a terrible thing.[9]

For stubborn stains the brush will not reach, try using a soft, small-pored sponge such as a makeup sponge works well or a bit of foam rubber. Rubber sponges are slightly sticky and will coax surface soiling away from the felt. An art-gum eraser will work as well, as long as you remember to rub with a counterclockwise motion to the grain.[10]

For deeper stains, sandpaper is required. Using the finest sandpaper on the market, move the sandpaper counterclockwise very gently and gently touch the dirty spot. Be careful not to dig in or to use your finger to push up against the spot from underneath as either of these will cause the sandpaper to dig in and create a weak spot. When sandpapering is required, make sure to remove only the tiniest layer of felt.[11]

Oily stains are a different matter. For these you need to head to the paint or drug store and find Fuller's Earth. It has the consistency of baking powder, will not stain hats, and will draw the oily residue out of the hat fibers. Brush the stained spot off first. Apply roughly one-eight inch worth of Fuller's Earth, and let it sit for two or three hours. Brush the powder off afterwards with a soft brush or towel. Repeat this process if necessary. When finished, use a plastic or rubber sponge to clean away powder that has penetrated into the felt.[12]

If stains remain after all of this, find a professional renovator for your hat. Heavy sweat stains, for example, need professional attention as they penetrate deep into the body of the felt.

Handling Hats

Proper handling will extend the life of your hat. Never touch the hat with dirty, oily hands or gloves. There is no quicker way to ruin your hat. Pick up the hat from underneath by both the front and back brim to maintain the shape and set of the brim. Resting a hat not on your head on a hat stand or block will make this operation easier.[13]

Avoid resting your hat on any flat surface, especially if it has a snap brim. To preserve the pitch, or scope, of the brim, the lower front of the brim should hang over the edge of any surface it is resting on. Hats left on table tops bow up in the front and back while bending the sides downward and forever deforming the shape of the brim. If need be, you can also rest a hat on its crown, provided you place it on a clean surface.[14]

With proper handling and care, a quality hat will remain a thing of beauty and a source of pride in any collection or on any head for years to come.

The cowboy hat remains an icon of the American West ... and the Stetson is *the* enduring definition of the cowboy hat. *Courtesy of Dick Engel.* NP

Conclusions

John B. Stetson accomplished some remarkable things. He manufactured western hats which would quickly become recognized icons of the American West. The very name "Stetson" would become synonymous with western hats. He organized a group of people seen by society at large as lazy, wandering, unreliable, "mad hatters" into a productive, loyal labor force. Within his lifetime, Stetson also developed a lasting reputation for manufacturing expensive, high quality hats. Modern Stetson hats still benefit from that enduring reputation today.

Collectors of vintage Stetson hats are faced with some interesting choices. There are men's and women's hats to choose from, western and dress hats, felt and straw hats, hats owned by famous individuals, and hats sold at well known shops. Furthermore, there are many interesting items associated with Stetson which are not hats at all. Among the many items the John B. Stetson Company produced over 105 years are hat boxes, blocks and flanges, posters, service awards, miniature hats, and Christmas gifts. All of these have their own appeal. I sincerely hope that this book has adequately illustrated the many possibilities. Happy hunting!

Endnotes

Introduction

1. The dates 1870-1970 cover the period of production for Stetson's 4th and Montgomery Street factory complex where most Stetson hats were produced. John B. Stetson first made hats in Philadelphia in 1865. The Stetson Company was incorporated in Philadelphia, Pennsylvania, in 1891. The company would close its doors forever by January 1971.

2. In recent years, however, the cloth baseball cap seems to have become the most common form of headwear. Colin McDowell. *Hats. Status, Style, and Glamour.* (New York: Rizzoli, 1992), 7.

3. Jody Shields. *Hats. A Stylish History and Collector's Guide.* (New York: Clarkson Potter/Publisher, 1991), 117.

4. Debbie Henderson. *Cowboys & Hatters: Bond Street, Sagebrush, & the Silver Screen.* (Yellow Springs, Ohio: Wild Goose Press, 1996), 5.

5. Ibid. 5.

6. Elbert Hubbard. *Little Journeys to the Homes of Great Business Men. John B. Stetson.* (Erie, New York: Roycrofters, 1911), 39.

7. *The Stetson Century 1865-1965.* (Philadelphia, Pennsylvania: John B. Stetson Company, 1965), 12; William Reynolds and Ritch Rand. *The Cowboy Hat Book.* (Salt Lake City, Utah: Gibbs Smith, Publisher, 1995), 10.

8. Judy, Crandall. *Cowgirls. Early Images and Collectibles.* (Atglen, Pennsylvania: Schiffer Publishing, 1994), 10, 42.

9. "$1,500 Stetson Hat Starts World Tour." *The Evening Bulletin.* August 20, 1955. *The Evening Bulletin* was a local Philadelphia newspaper.

10. "Stetson Hats, Buried For Forty Two Years, Unearthed. Skeletons of Two Montana Bandits Dug Up. Stetsons Still In Good Condition." *The Hat Box. The Hat Box. Employes Magazine of the John B. Stetson Company.* vol. V, no. VIII, (May 1924), 11.

11. *Stetson Hats the World Over. The Story of 50 Years of Stetson Foreign Business.* Philadelphia, Pennsylvania: John B. Stetson Company, 1927).

12. "Telling the Story of Stetson Hats by Window Cards. Advertising Department Announces Fall Campaign Window Cards More In Demand This Season." *The Hat Box. Employes Magazine of the John B. Stetson Company.* vol. V, no. XI., (August 1924).

13. Mr. John B. Stetson, personal conversation with author and letter to author, 3 February and 17 February 1996.

Chapter I. Stetson Hats and Their Methods of Manufacture

1. *Stetson Monthly.* Exposition Number. (Philadelphia, Pennsylvania: John B. Stetson Company, October 1899), 13; *The John B. Stetson Company Catalogue.* (Philadelphia, Pennsylvania: John B. Stetson Company, 1901); "John B. Stetson Company Holding Open House Tuesday and Wednesday for 3000 Workers, Families and Friends. 75 Years of Hats." *Philadelphia Record.* 15 December 1940.

2. The bowler was originally a working man's hat but was quickly adopted by the growing middle class. *Stetson Monthly,* October 1899, 13; *The John B. Stetson Company Catalogue,* 1901.

3. Ibid.

4. Ibid.

5. Reynolds and Rand, *The Cowboy Hat Book,* 23.

6. Ibid, 23-4.

7. *Stetson Monthly,* October 1899, 13; *John B. Stetson Company Catalogue,* 1901.

8. Reynolds and Rand, *The Cowboy Hat Book,* 26-7.

9. *John B. Stetson Company Catalogue,* 1901.

10. Reynolds and Rand, *The Cowboy Hat Book,* 27.

11. Shields, *A Stylish History and Collector's Guide,* 17.

12. *Hat Manufacture in Philadelphia.* (Issued by The Educational Committee of the Philadelphia Chamber of Commerce. Presented to the Schools of Philadelphia by John B. Stetson Company, 1922), 11.

13. Reynolds and Rand, *The Cowboy Hat Book,* 19.

14. Ibid, [the same page as the preceding note].

15. Ibid, 19-20.

16. In 1901 the individual labels shown in the text indicated various hat types sold at specific prices to retail outlets handling Stetsons: Premier and Nutria quality Stiff Hats—$39-$42 per dozen; Flexible Stiff Hats—$30 per dozen and upwards; B.O.P. style—$42 per dozen and upwards; 3X Beaver grade—$60 per dozen and upward; Grand Prize Paris 1900 Stiff Hats—$33 per dozen; Self-Conforming Stiff Hats—$30 per dozen; Clear Beaver—$72 per dozen and upwards; Stiff Hats (Stetson crest)—$30 per dozen and upwards; Real Nutria quality Soft Hats—$48 per dozen and upwards; Grand Prize Paris 1900 Flange Brims and Novelties—$39 per dozen and upwards; Nutria quality Soft Hats—$36 per dozen and upwards; and Star Flange Brims and Novelties—$30 per dozen and upwards. *The John B. Stetson Company Catalogue,* 1901.

17. Kristina Harris, *Vintage Fashions For Women. 1920s-1940s.* (Atglen, Pennsylvania: Schiffer Publishing, 1996), 24.

18. Mercury was used to "carrott" furs prior to making felt from them, poisoning many early hatters in the process (better ventilation and substitute chemicals would later cure this problem). This poisoning led to psychotic symptoms, hallucinations, and tremors in the victims. It also inspired the coinage of the phrase "mad as a hatter" by those who witnessed, and misinterpreted, the poisoned hatters' symptoms. McDowell. *Hats. Status, Style, and Glamour,* 58.

19. The steps involved in producing a Stetson felt hat, as described in this book, were all from pages 12-23 of Stetson's 1922 publication given to the Philadelphia school district. *Hat Manufacture in Philadelphia,* 11, 12-23.

Chapter II. The History of John B. Stetson and His Company

1. Hubbard, *Little Journeys to the Homes of Great Business Men*, 6-7; Tybie Moshinsky. "The Not So Mad Hatter." *Business Philadelphia*. (January 1991), 74-5; Henderson. *Cowboys and Hatters: Bond Street, Sagebrush, and the Silver Screen*, 25-6.
2. Hubbard, *Little Journeys to the Homes of Great Business Men*, 8-9.
3. William C. Reynolds. "Boss of the Plains. John B. Stetson and 130 Years of Hat Making." *Cowboys & Indians* (1995), 24-30.
4. Ibid. [The same pages as the preceding note.]
5. Ibid.
6. John L. Cotter, Daniel G. Roberts, and Michael Parrington. *The Buried Past. An Archaeological History of Philadelphia*. (Philadelphia, Pennsylvania: University of Pennsylvania Press, 1992), 57.
7. P. Herst & Co. was a large manufacturer of silk hats in Philadelphia during this period. The factory was located at 36 North Fifth Street and its founder invented a satin underbrim. *Hat Manufacture in Philadelphia*, 8.
8. In 1870, the values of annual hat manufactures had risen another quarter million dollars and by the 1920s the figure exceeded $13,000,000. *Hat Manufacture in Philadelphia*, 8.
9. Henderson, *Cowboys and Hatters: Bond Street, Sagebrush, and the Silver Screen*, 26.
10. John Anthony Scott. *The Story of America*. (Washington, D.C.: The National Geographic Society, 1984), 199-208.
11. Ibid. [The same pages as the preceding note.]
12. Tim Sheehy. "Stetson: The Hat that Won the West." *American Business* (June 1981); Reynolds, "Boss of the Plains. John B. Stetson and 130 Years of Hat Making," 24-30.
13. *Hat Manufacture in Philadelphia* (1922), 9.
14. John B. Stetson, letter to author, 27 February 1996.
15. Fredric M. Miller, Morris J. Vogel, and Allen F. Davis. *Still Philadelphia. A Photographic History, 1890-1940*. (Philadelphia, Pennsylvania: Temple University Press, 1983), 86.
16. From 1870-1890, the Stetson family's No Name Company enjoyed its greatest success. Its first president was John B. Stetson. It seems the hatting industry was very profitable in both Philadelphia, Pennsylvania and East Orange, New Jersey. Henderson, *Cowboys and Hatters: Bond Street, Sagebrush, and the Silver Screen*, 26; *The Stetson Century 1865-1965*.
17. *Stetson Monthly*, 3.
18. Moshinsky, "The Not So mad Hatter," 74-5.
19. "A Little Engine—Its Story of Stetson Progress. Relics of the Beginning of this Business Now an Interesting Exhibit in Boiler Room." *The Hat Box. Employes Magazine of the John B. Stetson Company*. (May 1925).
20. *Stetson Hats the World Over. The Story of 50 Years of Stetson Foreign Business* (Philadelphia, Pennsylvania: John B. Stetson Company, 1927).
21. Ibid.
22. *Stetson Monthly*, 2.
23. Ibid. [The same page as the preceding note.]
24. "John B. Stetson Company. Standard Hats." *Moody's Magazine*, February 1915.
25. "Stetson to Close Hat Store After 55 Years in Midcity." *The Evening Bulletin*, 7 April 1968.
26. Roman A. Cybriwsky and Charles Hardy III. "The Stetson Company and Benevolent Feudalism." *Pennsylvania Heritage*, Spring 1981, 14.
27. Today's John B. Stetson, the grand nephew of the company founder, states that he is the only Stetson who was actually born in the company hospital. John B. Stetson, letter to author, 27 February 1996; Cybriwsky and Hardy, "The Stetson Company and Benevolent Feudalism," 15.
28. Cybriwsky and Hardy, "The Stetson Company and Benevolent Feudalism," 15.
29. Ibid. [The same page as the preceding note.]
30. John B. Stetson, letter to author, 27 February 1996.
31. Ibid.
32. Stetson Christmas parties would continue throughout the decade of the 1920s, ending with the last party in 1930. In 1923, the total spent on gifts awarded was $559,155.60 and included the following: 412 Hats; 2813 Turkeys, total weight of 42,195 pounds; 1151 Pairs of Gloves; 1600 Pounds of Candy (received by women); 39 Watches and Chains (received by men); 360 Shares Building and Loan Stock; 260 Shares of John B. Stetson Co. Common Stock; 4 Life Insurance Policies of $5,000 each. "Many Employes Remembered at Christmas. Total Awards Amount to $559,155.60. Many Happy Surprises In List." *The Hat Box. Employes Magazine of the John B. Stetson Company*. vol. V, no. 11 (January 1924), 8.
33. Stetson followed in the footsteps of Henry Flagler and Henry Plant, who had recently "discovered" Florida and were building railroads and grand hotels in the state. In 1887, Stetson completed his three story DeLand mansion, built with Pennsylvania lumber on a 300 acre estate. It is stated that he spent one million dollars on the struggling DeLand Academy prior to its name change to Stetson University. Stetson spent every winter in DeLand for 20 years, dying there on February 18, 1906. Al Burt. "Mansion in the Middle. John B. Stetson, the hat tycoon, built it in all its three-storied, French-paneled glory back in 1887. Now its very existence is at stake, because it sits astride the zoning line between commercial and residential." *The Miami Herald* (5 October 1975).
34. These programs were also of great benefit to J.B. Stetson himself. In 1884, based on the success of his company, Stetson was able to build "Idro," a large mansion on Old York Road in Elkins Park outside of Philadelphia, for his third wife, Sara Elizabeth Shindler. By 1892 the house had 45 rooms, including some of the finest woodwork in the region. The dining room was finished in mahogany and lit by electric "bulls eyes" for soft lighting. Tiffany stained glass windows adorned the house, and additional rooms included a drawing room and a large library with a domed ceiling, bookcases built into the wall, and a stone fireplace. A large gym occupied part of the third floor where his sons John B. Jr. and George Henry played. In 1906, when John B. Stetson died at age 73, he left behind a fortune estimated between five and ten million dollars, and the house, to his 43 year old widow. Manning Smith. "Stetson Mansion Stands as Monument to Vain Hopes. There a Hoosier Farm Girl Cinderella Laid Her Plans to Become Portugal's Queen." *Philadelphia Record*. March 18, 1940.

35. "Compulsory Study to End Illiteracy." *The Evening Bulletin* (17 November 1921).

36. The American Civil War had spread interest in baseball across the fractured nation; soldiers played the game in camp. After the war, amateur and professional baseball clubs flourished. The first professional team was the Cincinnati Red Stockings, touring America in 1869. Russell F. Weigley (ed.). *Philadelphia. A 300-Year History*. (New York: W.W. Norton & Company, 1982), 458; Cybriwsky and Hardy, "The Stetson Company and Benevolent Feudalism," 14-20; "Stetson Athletic Field the Factory's Playground." *The Hat Box. Employes Magazine of the John B. Stetson Company*. (May 1925), 6.

37. One example of a children's activity put on by the company was recorded in *The Hat Box*. "Thursday Evening, May 21, 1925, the Stetson Kiddie Players will give another Calendrier Carnival in connection with our Annual Strawberry Festival. The Kiddie Players have broadcast a program a number of times during past year. They entertained a thousand kiddies at Woodside Park, gave their program at the Eastern Penitentiary for the prisoners and at the Pennsylvania Institute for the Blind at Overbrook, for the scholars and teachers. They have rehearsed every Saturday all winter ... Cards of admission, 35 cents, for the benefit of the Missionary Fund of the School. The ticket entitles you to Strawberries and Ice Cream in addition to the entertainment." "Calendrier Carnival and Strawberry Festival." *The Hat Box. Employes Magazine of the John B. Stetson Company*. (May 1925), 4.

38. One of the Stetson Company's long term employees was Antonio Salicondro of Mt. Holly, New Jersey. Mr. Salicondro, who died in 1969, was with the company for 52 years. He was to be one of the last handmade hat makers. He made and designed hats for celebrities including President Truman, Tom Mix, Arthur Godfrey, Hopalong Cassidy, and Andy Devine. He also developed Stetson's reinforced edge for hats. "Antonio Salicondro: Designed Truman Hat. Mt. Holly, NJ." Obituary, *The Evening Bulletin* (22 December 1969); Cybriwsky and Hardy, "The Stetson Company and Benevolent Feudalism," 14-20.

39. "John B. Stetson Co.'s Guaranteed Fur Hats." Montgomery Ward & Co.'s Catalogue, no. 29 (1910), 852.

40. One of the most vivid descriptions of what it must have been like to participate in the Philadelphia Centennial Exhibition was provided by the Japanese commissioner of the Exposition, Fukui Makota: "The first day crowds come like sheep, run here, run there, run everywhere. One man start, one thousand follow. Nobody can see anything, nobody can do anything. All rush, push, tear, shout, make plenty noise, say damn great many times, get very tired, and go home." Weigley, *Philadelphia. A 300-Year History*, 459-60.

41. *Stetson Monthly*, 4.

42. Ibid. [The same page as the preceding note.]

43. Cotter, et al., *The Buried Past. An Archaeological History of Philadelphia*, 68.

44. *The Hat Box. Employes Magazine of the John B. Stetson Company*. vol. V, no. 11 (January 1924).

45. J. Howell Cummings, Jr. "Survey Made of Rising Fur Costs. Increasing Demand for Skins in Many Markets and Weather Main Causes of Sharp Rise in Prices." *The Hat Box. Employes Magazine of the John B. Stetson Company*. (April 1925), 6; "Story of the Stetson Broadcast by Radio. Thousands of Listeners Hear Mr. Milton D. Gehris Discuss Our Product." *The Hat Box. Employes Magazine of the John B. Stetson Company*. (December 1925), 3-4. It is interesting to note that during this radio show, Mr. Gehris felt it necessary to make the following disclaimer concerning the 40,000 gallons of denatured alcohol required to make the shellac used to stiffen Stetson hats during Prohibition: "By the way, this use of alcohol, while it goes to the head is not in the least injurious and not contrary to the 18th Amendment."

46. "How Stetson Hats Are Displayed by Salesmen. Temporary Headquarters Made Attractive As Possible. Critical Buyers Watch All Details." *The Hat Box. Employes Magazine of the John B. Stetson Company*. vol. V, no. 11 (November 1923).

47. *The Hat Box. Employes Magazine of the John B. Stetson Company*. vol. V, no. VIII (May 1924).

48. "Hat Firm Gives City Reputation As a Millinery Center of the World." *The Evening Bulletin* (20 October 1952).

49. "Stetson Acquires Canada Hat Firms." [unidentified Philadelphia newspaper clipping] (12 March 1935).

50. In the court decision against the Stephen L. Stetson Company, Ltd., figures used to prove that the J.B. Stetson Company should have the sole right to the Stetson trademark included: between 1891 and 1935 J.B. Stetson sold 7,422,522 dozen hats with an invoice value of over $340,000,000 and produced roughly $5,000,000 worth of advertising materials. John B. Stetson Company, Philadelphia, 1936 [company pamphlet explaining the court decision]; "J.B. Stetson Wins Trade Name Suit." [unidentified Philadelphia newspaper clipping] (17 August 1936).

51. Ibid.

52. "He High-Hatted the West. Stetson's '10-gallon' Swept Plains." [unidentified Philadelphia newspaper clipping] (May 1939); News photograph from an unidentified Philadelphia newspaper with attached copy found at Temple University (3 March 1940).

53. Cybriwsky and Hardy, "The Stetson Company and Benevolent Feudalism," 14-20.

54. Ibid. [The same pages as the preceding note.]; Moshinsky, "The Not So Mad Hatter," 74-5; "Stetson Labor Dispute Ended. Company Grants Union's Demand for Recognition." [unidentified Philadelphia newspaper clipping] (1 September 1936).

55. Ibid.

56. Moshinsky, "The Not So Mad Hatter," 74-5.

57. "7 Bids Received on U.S. Army Hats. John B. Stetson Co. & Paul B. Hendel made low offers." *The Evening Bulletin* (16 November 1940).

58. "Stetson to Raze 9 Buildings for 4000 Tons Scrap" [unidentified Philadelphia newspaper clipping] (17 May 1943); "Landmark Goes; A Double Saving." [unidentified Philadelphia newspaper clipping] (8 June 1943); telephone conversation with William R. Morris.

59. "Stetson Acquires Mallory Hat Co. Change of ownership to have no immediate effect on companies' operations." [unidentified Philadelphia newspaper clipping] (17 August 1946); "Stetson Holds on to Its Hat As Signs Point to Sales Gain." *The Evening Bulletin* (9 March 1958).

60. Cotter, et al., *The Buried Past. An Archaeological History of Philadelphia*, 71.

61. "1224 Chestnut Brings $345,000. Prudential Insurance Purchases Building." *The Evening Bulletin* (21 July 1950); "Hat Firm Gives City Reputation As a Millinery Center of the World." *The Evening Bulletin* (20 October 1952).

62. "Stetson Holds on to Its Hat As Signs Point to Sales Gain." *The Evening Bulletin* (9 March 1958).

63. David Harshaw. *Annual Stock Report* (Philadelphia, Pennsylvania: John B. Stetson Company, January 18, 1965), 4.

64. Ibid. [The same page as the preceding note.]

65. In early 1968, the Stetson Company also operated Stetson retail stores in New York City, Philadelphia, Chester, and Pittsburgh, Pennsylvania, Buffalo, New York, Chicago, Illinois, Seattle, Washington, and South Weymouth, Massachusetts. "Company Portraits. John B. Stetson." *The Evening Bulletin* (14 December 1968); "J.B. Stetson Co. Buys N.Y. Hat Store Chain." *The Evening Bulletin* (12 January 1955); "Stetson Purchases Neckwear Firm." *The Evening Bulletin* (5 January 1956); "Stetson Co. Acquires The Fuller Shirt Co." *The Evening Bulletin* (31 December 1956); "J.B. Stetson Co. Purchases Outstanding Stock in Frank Lee." *The Evening Bulletin* (16 July 1960); "J.B. Stetson Buys N.Y. Hat Manufacturer." *The Evening Bulletin* (23 September 1968).

66. "J.B. Stetson Co. Announced Today is Reentering Women's Hat Business." *The Evening Bulletin* (24 May 1965).

67. "Stetson to Close Hat Store After 55 Years in Midcity." *The Evening Bulletin* (7 April 1968); "Too Many in Ring. Free Hats Ruled Out." *The Evening Bulletin* (10 March 1969).

68. A smoldering resentment remains among some Philadelphians who were employed or on pensions in those final years. John W. McGraw, head of the Local 60 union at Stetson admitted shortly before the plant closed that the union would have a hard time finding work for the remaining employees, their average ages ranged from the late 50s to early 60s. He also stated that pensioners in 1970 had taken a 62% cut in payments early in the year and it was likely they would be cut off altogether. Pensions were cut off and over 25 years later families are still angry. "Stetson to Quit Making Hats At Plant Here. Union to Bargain To Affirm Rights of 300 Employes. Stetson to give up hatmaking - John B. Stetson hat company, founded by John Batterson Stetson 105 years ago in Philadelphia, plans to abandon hatmaking early in 1971." [unidentified newspaper clipping] (31 December 1970).

69. Philip A. Roth. "President's Letter." *Annual Stock Report.* (24 March 1971), 9.

70. In 1980, the company reported that John B. Stetson's son G. Henry Stetson would not stand for reelection to the board of directors, upon which he had served since 1935. He received the title of Director Emeritus as he stepped down. *John B. Stetson Company Annual Report for 1979.* (20 February 1980), 2-3; Newspaper photograph by Michael J. Maicker with accompanying copy, "Old Stetson Hat Factory being demolished ... 5th & Germantown Ave." (8 March 1979); "The Crash of the Past Making Way." *The Evening Bulletin.* (4 May 1979).

71. Pat Guy. "She Keeps Hat On Through Tough Times." *USA Today* (1986).

72. Scott Kraft. "A New Generation is Bringing the 'Boss of the Plains' Off the Prairie." *Star Sentinel* [Florida newspaper] (22 April 1979).

73. Ibid.

74. Tim Sheehy. "Stetson: The Hat that Won the West." *American Business* (June 1981); Moshinsky, "The Not So Mad Hatter," 74-5.

75. Reynolds and Rand, *The Cowboy Hat Book*, 38-43.

Chapter III. Men's Hats

1. McDowell, *Hats. Status, Style and Glamour,* 220-221.
2. *Stetson Monthly* (October 1899); *Montgomery Ward & Co. Catalogue* (Fall and Winter 1900-1901), 1061.
3. *Montgomery Ward & Co. Catalogue* (Fall and Winter 1900-1901), 1061.
4. Ibid. [The same page as the preceding note.]
5. McDowell, *Hats. Status, Style and Glamour,* 220-221.
6. *Montgomery Ward & Co. Catalogue* (Fall and Winter 1910), 852.
7. Ibid. [The same page as the preceding note.]
8. Ibid.
9. Ibid.
10. Ibid.
11. Ibid.
12. Ibid.
13. Ibid.
14. Ibid.
15. Ibid.
16. Ibid.
17. Ibid.
18. Ibid.
18a. Ibid.
19. Ibid.
20. McDowell, *Hats. Status, Style and Glamour,* 220-221.
21. *Stockman-Farmer Supply Co.* Catalog no. 32, (Spring 1928), 4.
22. Ibid. [The same page as the preceding note.]
23. Ibid.
24. Ibid.
25. Ibid.
26. Ibid.
27. "A Stetson Hat Saved Him From Jail." *The Hat Box. Employes Magazine of the John B. Stetson Company.* (May 1925), 3.
28. McDowell, *Hats. Status, Style and Glamour,* 220-221.
29. McDowell, *Hats. Status, Style and Glamour,* 220-221; "John B. Stetson Company Holding Open House Tuesday and Wednesday for 3000 Workers, Families and Friends. 75 Years of Hats." *Philadelphia Record* (15 December 1940).
30. "John B. Stetson Company Holding Open House Tuesday and Wednesday for 3000 Workers, Families and Friends. 75 Years of Hats." *Philadelphia Record* (15 December 1940).
31. Ibid.
32. McDowell, *Hats. Status, Style and Glamour,* 220-221.
33. Ibid. [The same page as the preceding note.]

34. Martin J. Herman. "Once Aristocrat of Bluecollar Jobs, Hatmaker's Lot Is Not a Happy One." *The Evening Bulletin* (n.d.).
35. McDowell, *Hats. Status, Style and Glamour*, 220-221.
36. Nugent Robinson (compiler). *Collier's Cyclopedia of Commercial and Social Information and Treasury of Useful and Entertaining Knowledge.* (New York: P. F. Collier, 1882), 622-34.
37. McDowell, *Hats. Status, Style and Glamour,* 100.
38. Ibid. [The same page as the preceding note.]
39. Reynolds and Rand, *The Cowboy Hat Book*, 89.
40. McDowell, *Hats. Status, Style and Glamour,* 97.
41. McDowell, *Hats. Status, Style and Glamour,* 100.
42. "Judging a Man by the Way He Wears His Stetson. Stetson Booklet Explains Character Analysis Based on Mode of Wearing Hat." *The Hat Box. Employes Magazine of the John B. Stetson Company.* vol. 5, no. 6 (March 1924), 7.
43. McDowell, *Hats. Status, Style and Glamour,* 104.

Chapter IV. Women's Hats

1. McDowell, *Hats. Status, Style and Glamour*, 220-221.
2. Ibid. [The same pages as the preceding note.]
3. *Stetson Monthly* (October 1899).
4. McDowell, *Hats. Status, Style and Glamour*, 220-221.
5. Ibid. [The same pages as the preceding note.]
6. Ibid.
7. Ibid.
8. Ibid.
9. Ibid.
10. Ibid.
11. Ibid.
12. Desire Smith. *Hats.* (Atglen, Pennsylvania: Schiffer Publishing, 1996), 128.

Chapter V. Care of Hats

1. Robert W.D. Ball and Ed Vebell. *Cowboy Collectibles and Western Memorabilia* (West Chester, Pennsylvania: Schiffer Publishing, 1991), 17.
2. Shields, *Hats. A stylish history and collector's guide*, 119.
3. Ibid. [The same page as the preceding note.]
4. Ibid.
5. Ibid.
6. Ibid.
7. Ibid. 119-120; Reynolds and Rand, *The Cowboy Hat Book*, 29.
8. Reynolds and Rand, *The Cowboy Hat Book*, 29, 34.
9. Ibid. 29.
10. Ibid. [The same page as the preceding note.]
11. Ibid.
12. Ibid. 29-30.
13. Ibid. 31-32.
14. Ibid. 32-34.

Bibliography

Books & Magazine Articles

Ball, Robert W.D. & Ed Vebell. *Cowboy Collectibles and Western Memorabilia*. West Chester, Pennsylvania: Schiffer Publishing, 1991.

"Camp Cook Wins Stetson." *The Hat Box. Employes Magazine of the John B. Stetson Company* (November 1925).

"Colonel 'Bill Pearson' Visits Our Factory. Famous Cowboy, Friend of Buffalo Bill, Makes Two-Day Stay Meeting All the Executives and Many Workers of Plant." *The Hat Box. Employes Magazine of the John B. Stetson Company*. 5(3) (December 1923).

Cotter, John L., Daniel G. Roberts, and Michael Parrington. *The Buried Past. An Archaeological History of Philadelphia*. Philadelphia, Pennsylvania: University of Pennsylvania Press, 1992.

Crandall, Judy. *Cowgirls. Early Images and Collectibles*. Atglen, Pennsylvania: Schiffer Publishing, 1994.

Cybriwsky, Roman A. & Charles Hardy III. "The Stetson Company and Benevolent Feudalism." *Pennsylvania Heritage* (Spring 1981).

Guy, Pat. "She keeps hat on through tough times." *USA Today*. (1986)

Harris, Kristina. *Vintage Fashions For Women. 1920s-1940s*. Atglen, Pennsylvania: Schiffer Publishing, 1996.

Harshaw, David. "President's Message To The Shareholders." *Annual Stock Report, John B. Stetson Company* (18 January 1965).

Hat Manufacture in Philadelphia. Issued by The Educational Committee of the Philadelphia Chamber of Commerce. Presented to the Schools of Philadelphia by John B. Stetson Company, 1922.

Henderson, Debbie. *Cowboys and Hatters: Bond Street, Sagebrush, and the Silver Screen*. Yellow Springs, Ohio: Wild Goose Press, 1996.

Hubbard, Elbert. *Little Journeys to the Homes of Great Business Men. John B. Stetson*. Erie, New York: Roycrofters, 1911.

John B. Stetson Company Annual Report for 1979 (February 20, 1980).

The John B. Stetson Company Catalogue. 1901.

John B. Stetson Company, Philadelphia, U.S.A. Document concerning a court decision against the Stephen L. Stetson Company, Ltd., 1936.

"John B. Stetson Company. Standard Hats." *Moody's Magazine* (February 1915).

John B. Stetson (grand nephew of the firm's founder), personal conversation with author, 3 February 1996, and letter to author, 17 February 1996.

"Judging a Man by the Way He Wears His Stetson." *The Hat Box. Employes Magazine of the John B. Stetson Company* 5(6) (March 1924).

"A Little Engine—Its Story of Stetson Progress. Relics of the Beginning of this Business Now an Interesting Exhibit in Boiler Room." *The Hat Box. Employes Magazine of the John B. Stetson Company* (May 1925).

McCutcheon, Marc. *The Writer's Guide to Everyday Life in the 1800s*. Cincinnati, Ohio: Writer's Digest Books, 1993.

McDowell, Colin. *Hats. Status, Style and Glamour*. New York: Rizzoli, 1992.

Miller, Fredric M., Morris J. Vogel, and Allen F. Davis. *Still Philadelphia. A Photographic History, 1890-1940*. Philadelphia, Pennsylvania: Temple University Press, 1983.

Moshinsky, Tybie. "The Not So Mad Hatter." *Business Philadelphia* (January 1991).

Reynolds, William and Ritch Rand. *The Cowboy Hat Book*. Salt Lake City, Utah: Gibbs Smith, Publisher, 1995.

Reynolds, William C. "Boss of the Plains. John B. Stetson and 130 Years of Hat Making." *Cowboys & Indians* (1995).

Robinson, Nugent (compiler). *Collier's Cyclopedia of Commercial and Social Information and Treasury of Useful and Entertaining Knowledge*. New York: P. F. Collier, 1882.

Roth, Philip A. "President's Letter." *Annual Stock Report, John B. Stetson Company* (March 24, 1971).

Scott, John Anthony. *The Story of America*. Washington, D.C.: The National Geographic Society, 1984.

Sheehy, Tim. "Stetson: The Hat that Won the West." *American Business* (June 1981).

Shields, Jody. *Hats. A Stylish History and Collector's Guide.* New York: Clarkson Potter/Publishers, 1991.

Smith, Desire. *Hats.* Atglen, Pennsylvania: Schiffer Publishing, 1996.

The Stetson Century 1865-1965. Philadelphia, Pennsylvania: John B. Stetson Company, 1965.

"Stetson Hats, Buried For Forty Two Years, Unearthed. Skeletons of Two Montana Bandits Dug Up. Stetsons Still In Good Condition." *The Hat Box. Employes Magazine of the John B. Stetson Company.* 5(8) (May 1924).

"A Stetson Hat Saved Him From Jail." *The Hat Box. Employes Magazine of the John B. Stetson Company* (May 1925).

Stetson Hats the World Over. The Story of 50 Years of Stetson Foreign Business. Philadelphia, Pennsylvania: J.B. Stetson Co., 1927.

Stetson Monthly. Exposition Number. Philadelphia, Pennsylvania: John B. Stetson Company, 1899.

Stettel, Irving. *A Pictorial History of Radio.* New York: Grosset & Dunlap, 1960.

Stockman-Farmer Supply Co. Denver, Colorado: Catalog No. 32. (Spring 1928), 4.

"Story of the Stetson Broadcast by Radio. Thousands of Listeners Hear Mr. Milton D. Gehris Discuss Our Product." *The Hat Box. Employes Magazine of the John B. Stetson Company* (December 1925).

"Telling the Story of Stetson Hats by Window Cards. Advertising Department Announces Fall Campaign Window Cards More In Demand This Season." *The Hat Box. Employes Magazine of the John B. Stetson Company* 5(11) (August 1924).

Weigley, Russell F. (ed.). *Philadelphia. A 300-Year History.* New York: W.W. Norton & Company, 1982.

Newspaper Articles

The Evening Bulletin, Philadelphia, Pennsylvania: November 16, 1940, July 21, 1950, October 20, 1952, January 12, 1955, August 20, 1955, January 5, 1956, December 31, 1956, March 9, 1958, July 16, 1960, May 24, 1965, January 5, 1966, April 7, 1968, September 23, 1968, December 14, 1968, March 10, 1969, October 12, 1969, November 6, 1969, December 22, 1969, August 23, 1970, January 11, 1971, January 25, 1971, May 4, 1979.

The New York Times: December 6, 1970.

The News-Times: March 3, 1974.

Philadelphia Record: March 18, 1940, December 15, 1940.

Sentinel Star, Florida: April 22, 1979.

Unidentified Philadelphia, Pennsylvania, Paper Clippings: (found in the files of the Temple University Business Archives and the Hagley Museum Library) December 25, 1929, April 5, 1932, March 12, 1935, July 14, 1936, August 17, 1936, September 1, 1936, August 8, 1937, August 21, 1938, May 1939, March 3, 1940, May 17, 1943, June 8, 1943, August 17, 1946, December 29, 1946, December 31, 1970, March 8, 1979.

United Press International: June 11, 1985.

Wilmington Morning News, Delaware: September 20, 1972.

Appendix

These were the holdings of the John B. Stetson Company at the time the Philadelphia factory was closed. These listings appeared in the *President's Letter* in the *Annual Stock Report* dated March 24, 1971. Ira Guilden was the chairman of the board and Philip A. Roth was the company president.

Locations of various Stetson operations:
   General Executive Offices: Fifth Street and Montgomery Avenue. Philadephia.
   Felt Hat Division. Philadelphia. Danbury, Connecticut.
   Straw Hat Division. Philadelphia.
   United Fur Cutters Division. Newark, New Jersey.
   Neckware Division. Philadelphia.
   Shirt Division. Philadelphia.
   G.W. Alexander & Co. Inc. Reading, Pennsylvania
   Stetson Shoe Company, Inc. South Weymouth, Massachusetts
   John B. Stetson Company (Canada) Limited. Brockville, Ontario

Sales Offices:
U.S.
Atlanta, Atlanta Merchandise Mart
Chicago, Merchandise Mart
Dallas, Adolphus Tower
Los Angeles, 510 W. Sixth Street
New York, Fifth Avenue at 48th Street
Philadelphia, Fifth St. and Montgomery Ave.

Canada
Calgary, Grain Exchange Building
Montreal, Birks Building
Quebec, 771 Rue St. Joseph E.
Saskatoon, 209 Glengarry Block
Toronto, Hyslop Building
Vancouver, 367 Water Street
Winnipeg, Norlyn Building

Retail Stores
New York, Fifth Avenue at 48th Street
Philadelphia, 1224 Chestnut Street
Pittsburgh, 445 Wood Street
Buffalo, 305 Main Street

International Division
Foreign Licensees
Australia, Dunkerley Hat Mills Limited
Brazil, Industrias Dante Ramenzoni, S. A.
Colombia, Pan American Hat Co., S. A.
Finland, AB Silfverbergs & Wecksells
Germany, Mayser's Hutfabrik
Great Britain, Failsworth Hats Limited
Guatemala, Fabrica de Sombreros de Fieltro Tardan
Ireland, Western Hats Ltd.
Japan, Tokyo Hat Co., Ltd.
Mexico, Sombrereros Unidos S. A.
New Zealand, Ross & Glendining Ltd.
Norway, Nordisk Hattefabrik A-S
South Africa, Dorian Hats (Pty.) Ltd.

Index

A

Advertising art, 20
Alaska, men's western hat, 73, 74
Apprenticeships, 55
Austin, men's western hat, 27
Autry, Gene, 10, 11

B

Baden-Powell, men's western hat, 26, 27
Baden-Powell, R.S.S., 10
Big Four, men's western hat, 81
Bindings, 30
Blesing, Faye Johnson, 10
Block, 8, 22,
Boater, men's straw dress hat, 27, 79
Boss of the Plains, men's western hat, 5, 9, 27, 29, 49-51, 73, 74
Boss Raw Edge Kettle Finish, 31
Bowler, men's dress hat, 27-28, 60, 75, 76, 77, 79, 83, 130
Boxes, hat, 14-19
Boxes, hat, miniature, 23-25
Brim, definition, 8
Brims, hat, 29-30

C

Caps, Stetson, 80
Carlsbad, men's western hat, 81
Carrotting, 40
Catalogs
    Montgomery Ward & Company, 60, 73-74, 75
    Sears, Roebuck & Company, 11, 74, 80, 82, 83, 89, 90, 136-137, 140-141, 150-151, 172-173
    Stetson, 52, 72
    Stockman-Farmer Supply Company, 81

Character and class among hat wearers, 130-131
Charlie 1 Horse, 71
Christmas parties, company, 22, 57, 66, 179
Cody, William F., Colonel, 10
Color, felt, 27, 83
Color, straw, 83
Columbia, men's western hat, 73, 74
Conspicuous consumption, 132
Coypu, 8, *see also Nutria*.
Crease, definition, 8
Crown, definition, 8
Cummings, J. Howell, 58

D

Dakota, men's western hat, 73, 74
Dilworth, Richardson, 12
Diversification, 69
Doffing the hat, 129-130
Dormont, Philip, 84-85, 87, 88
Dress makers, 62

E

Edward, Prince of Wales, 27, 73
Employee benefits, 55, 66
Employees, 59, 65-67, 70, 181
Etiquette, hat wearing, 129-130

F

Fedora, men's dress hat, 9, 13, 27-28, 73, 75, 76, 80
Felt, 7, 33
Finishes, 31
Flange, 8, 22

H

Harshaw, David H., 69
Hat Box, The, 20-21, 58, 79, 82
Hat Brands, Inc., 71
Hat care, 174-175
Hat forms, 8
Hat materials, 8
Hat terminology, 8
Hat wearing, decline of, 64, 68-71, 89, 90, 142
Hatbands, 32
Hats as gifts, 10, 13
Hats
    cloth, 90
    dress, 26, 84-88
    dust removal, 175
    Featherweight, 28
    flexible, 28
    for American Presidents, 62
    for International Dignitaries, 62-63
    handling, 175
    manufacture, 40-47
    men's 72-131
    men's dress, 120-128
    men's western, 7, 8, 13, 14, 49, 78, 91-119, 176
    qualities, trademarks, and labels, 32-39
    self-conforming, 28
    stain removal, 175
    staple (western), 26, 72, 73
    stiff, 28, 83
    women's, 69, 84-88, 132-173
    women's feathered, 171
    women's floral, 168
    women's Freedom Fashions, 139
    women's straw, 143-149, 159
    women's velveteen, 160-162, 164-165
    women's western, 132, 133
Hatter's Highlights, 67
Homburg, men's dress hat, 12, 27, 75
Hutt and Wasserman, Inc., 65

I

Immigrants, 55, 59
Immigration restriction acts, 62
International business, 52-53
International Exhibitions, 39, 61, 180
International Stetson factories, 64
Iron hats, 50

J

Jape, playing the, 131
John B. Stetson Company, 6, 15, 50-71, 83, 91, 173
John B. Stetson University, 58, 179
Jones, Buck, 79

L

Licensees
    domestic, 70-71, 91
    foreign, 70
Licensing the Stetson name, 68-71
Lincoln, men's western hat, 27
Linings, hat, 31
Lone Star, men's western hat, 81

M

Mad hatters, 177, 178
Mallory Hat Company, 68
Middle class, 72
Millinery Department, 64, 67, 69, 70, 132, 134, 140, 174
Mix, Tom, 10, 11, 62, 79, 180
Montana Peak, men's western hat, 91

N

No Name Hat Company, 48
Novelty, men's dress hats, 29, 77-78
Nutria, 8, 13, 26

O

Open Road, men's western hat, 10, 12

P

Panama, men's dress hat, 27, 75, 79
Paternalism, 55-60
Paternalism, end of, 66
Post-War Boom of 1947, 68
Posters, 20
Profile, definition, 8
Prohibition, 180

R

Railroad, men's western hat, 73, 74
Railroads, 50
Resistol, 71
Retail merchants, 53
Roach, Ruth, 10, 11
Rodeo riders, 10, 11
Rogers, Roy, 10, 12

S

Salesmen, 131
Salicondro, Antonio, 180
San An, men's western hat, 81
Scope, definition, 8
Silhouette, definition, 8
Snap brim, men's dress hat, 27, 83
Stephen L. Stetson Company, Ltd., 65, 180
Stetson Building and Loan Association, 56
Stetson Fifth Avenue Store, 70
Stetson Hat Company Group, 71, 91
Stetson Mission Chapel, 66-67
Stetson retail shops and offices, 17, 54, 62, 95, 181
Stetson Retail Store, Philadelphia, 17, 53, 64, 69, 70, 82
Stetson Shoe Company, Inc., 69
Stetson, George Arthur, 51, 56
Stetson, George Henry, 179, 181
Stetson, John Batterson, 9, 48-58, 177
Stetson, John Batterson, Jr., 179
Stetson, Stephen, 48
Stetson, Willis George, 22, 56
Stevens Hat Company, 71
Surprise, men's western hat, 81
Sweatband, definition, 8, 32

T

Trilby or snap brim, men's dress hat, 27, 73, 75, 79, 82

U

Union Mission Hospital, 56
Unionization, 66
United Hatters, Cap and Millinery Workers International Union, 66, 90

W

Whiteman, Paul, 12
Window cards, 20
Wolthausen Hat Corporation, 64-65
World War I, 62
World War II, 66-67